DID YOU GET THE GIFT?

HOW GRATITUDE LEADS TO CONTENTMENT, CALMNESS, AND CELEBRATION

BY

SYAVIHA MULENGYA

This book is a gift

From:_____

To:_____

On:_____

Personal Comments

_____

_____

_____

_____

_____

Thank you God for your goodness, grace
and the gift you have bestowed upon me

DEDICATION

- To my late parents, Samuel Mahamba and Elizabeth Vahingania, thank you for loving, listening and leading me in the ways of God.

- My brothers and sisters, Moise, Samson, Schandrack, Semu, Seriba, Yerusi, Desize, Kahambu and Katungu Mulengya, thank you for teaching me the values of hope, humility and hard work.

- To my mentors, Janine and Sid Phillips, thank you for your inspiration, instruction and information. You always encourage and believe in my vision.

- To Devin and Christine Walker, you have motivated me to serve, seek and stay close to God. Thank you for your wisdom and the great work you are doing.

- To my queen Rafiki Kavuya Syaviha, thank you for standing, supporting and serving with me in hard and good times. You are my miracle.

- To my lovely daughters, Blessed and Best and Brilliance, you always encourage, excite and enjoy my work. You are my greatest inspiration.

- To my friends and fans, you always advise, appreciate and assist me in this noble work. Thank you for the financial support.

Table of Content

INTRODUCTION

What Is *Did You Get the Gifts?* About?

Gratitude is more than a feeling—it's a way of life. *Did You Get the Gifts?* invites you to pause and recognize the blessings that surround you every single day. These gifts may not always arrive in comfort, but they carry the touch of God. You've been given breath to rise, peace to rest, purpose to pursue, and people to walk beside you. None of these came by accident—they are signs of divine love. Each sunrise is a reminder that you've been trusted with another day. Every moment whispers that your life matters. The Bible says, "Every good and perfect gift is from above" (James 1:17), and that includes the ones you didn't ask for but truly needed. This book will help you see what's already in your hands and what's waiting in your heart. It will gently guide you to unwrap the spiritual treasures hidden in your journey. You'll begin to see with new eyes and feel with a grateful heart.

Gratitude will shape how you live, how you speak, and how you see the world. It will become your lens for joy, your language of peace, and your lifestyle of praise. When you begin to notice the gifts, you'll walk with confidence and calm. When you receive with thanksgiving, you'll grow in grace and goodness. When you praise God as you walk, work, and wake up, your life becomes a testimony of hope. Gratitude will help you build a life that is happy, healthy, hopeful, and harmonious. It will remind you that every day is precious and every breath is sacred. You'll stop chasing what's missing and start cherishing what's present. Let gratitude be part of you—woven into your thoughts, your prayers, and your purpose. As you grow in gratitude, you'll grow in strength. As you live with thanksgiving, you'll live with joy. And as you honor the gifts, you'll discover the Giver in every step.

Complaining comes quickly. Comparing happens often. But gratitude—gratitude is powerful. It lifts your eyes from what's missing to what's meaningful. You've walked through pain, but you've also been carried by grace. You've faced loss, yet love found you in the dark. Gratitude doesn't erase the struggle—it gives it purpose. The Bible says, "Give thanks in all circumstances, for this is God's will for you in Christ Jesus" (1 Thessalonians 5:18). That means even in the valley, you can still lift your voice. Gratitude is not denial—it's declaration. It says, "God is still good, even here." You're invited to rediscover joy that doesn't depend on circumstances. You're called to restore peace that passes understanding. You're ready to renew strength that you thought was gone.

Gratitude will shift your focus and soften your heart. It will help you see beauty in broken places and miracles in mundane moments. You'll begin to notice what you've overlooked and appreciate what you've undervalued. You'll stop measuring your life by what you lack and start celebrating what you carry. Gratitude will teach you to pause, reflect, and rejoice. It will help you see your story through the lens of grace. You'll learn to thank God not just for what He gives, but for who He is. Gratitude will become your rhythm, your refuge, and your reason to keep going. It will help you walk with peace, speak with kindness, and live with clarity. You'll begin to see that every moment matters and every breath is sacred. Gratitude will not just change your mood—it will transform your

SYAVIHA MULENGYA

mindset. And when your perspective shifts, your whole life begins to shine.

Every day is a gift. Every breath is a blessing. Gratitude will teach you to celebrate small victories and honor quiet moments. You'll begin to see divine surprises in ordinary places. You'll stop rushing past miracles and start resting in them. Gratitude will become your anchor in storms and your song in silence. It will help you build a life that is happy, healthy, hopeful, and harmonious. You won't just read—you'll reflect, respond, and rise. You'll begin to live with eyes wide open and a heart full of praise. You'll stop waiting for perfect days and start worshiping in imperfect ones. Gratitude will help you embrace the now and trust God with the next. You'll learn to say, "This day is enough, and I am grateful."

Today is not just another date on the calendar—it's a divine appointment. You've been given this moment to breathe, believe, and build. Gratitude will help you wake up with wonder and walk with wisdom. You'll begin to see that time is sacred and presence is powerful. The Bible says, "This is the day the Lord has made; let us rejoice and be glad in it" (Psalm 118:24). Gratitude will help you rejoice even when the day feels heavy. It will help you find joy in the journey and peace in the process. You'll stop living in regret and start living in revelation. Gratitude will help you honor the gift of now and prepare your heart for what's ahead. When you receive today with thanksgiving, you begin to live with purpose. And when you live with purpose, you walk in peace.

Breath and Belonging are gifts. You've received more than you realize. Gratitude will help you uncover the blessings that often go unnoticed. You'll discover the gift of waking up with purpose, walking in peace, and working with joy. You'll see how God uses both laughter and loss to shape your soul. The Bible says, "He gives strength to the weary and increases the power of the weak" (Isaiah 40:29). That means even when you feel empty, you're not without grace. Gratitude will help you treasure relationships, honor your story, and recognize divine provision. You'll begin to say, "Yes, I got the gifts—and I'm grateful." You'll stop chasing what's next and start cherishing what's now.

Breath is not just oxygen—it's opportunity. Every inhale is a reminder that you're still here, still chosen, still loved. Gratitude will help you breathe deeper and live fuller. You'll begin to see your life as a miracle in motion. You'll stop taking moments for granted and start treating them as sacred. Gratitude will help you slow down and listen, reflect and rejoice. You'll learn to thank God for the breath that carries your prayers and the strength that carries your steps. You'll begin to live with awareness, walk with appreciation, and speak with affirmation. Gratitude will help you see that your breath is borrowed from heaven. And when you breathe with thanksgiving, you live with intention.

Bitterness will break. Confusion will clear. Gratitude has the power to heal what pain has buried. When your heart feels heavy and your spirit feels dry, thanksgiving becomes the turning point. Emotional exhaustion may have drained your joy, but gratitude will refill your soul. Spiritual disconnection may have silenced your song, but praise will bring it back. The Bible says, "Enter his gates with thanksgiving and his courts with praise" (Psalm 100:4). That means healing begins when you choose to thank God, even in the middle of the mess. Gratitude is not just a response—it's a remedy. It opens the door to peace, even when your past feels loud. You'll begin to feel again, believe again, and breathe again. You'll stop defining your life by what you've lost and start celebrating what you've gained. You'll remember who you are and reclaim what you carry.

SYAVIHA MULENGYA

Gratitude helps you move from feeling hopeless to feeling whole. It brings back your joy, gives you new strength, and lifts your spirit. Life becomes more meaningful, not just full of pressure, but full of purpose. Instead of just surviving, you begin to thrive. You stop living in the past and start stepping into today with faith. A thankful heart builds a life that is happy, healthy, hopeful, and full of peace. Even in hard times, you start to see beauty and find strength. Gratitude teaches you to thank God not only for what He gives, but also for how He helps you grow. Regret loses its grip, and you begin to walk in freedom. You stop wondering if you missed the gifts and start saying, "I received them—and I'm ready to share them." Healing begins when you choose to be thankful. And when you welcome both grace and gratitude, your life becomes a story of hope and change.

Gratitude is a gift that changes everything. When you choose to be thankful, you unlock the door to peace, joy, and strength. Gratitude is not just a feeling—it's a decision, a lifestyle, and a spiritual weapon. In this book Did You Get The Gift?, we explore how gratitude leads to contentment, calmness, and celebration. You'll learn how to grow in goodness and grace by simply saying "thank you" more often. Life is full of challenges, but gratitude helps you see the blessings hidden in every moment. It shifts your focus from what's missing to what's meaningful. It helps you stop worrying and start worshiping. Gratitude brings healing to your heart and clarity to your mind. It lifts your spirit and strengthens your faith. When you grow with gratitude, you grow with God. And when you grow with God, you grow in goodness. *"Give thanks to the Lord, for He is good; His love endures forever."* —Psalm 107:1

Contentment begins with a grateful heart. Many people chase happiness but never find it. They search for peace in possessions, positions, or popularity. But true contentment comes from within—
SYAVIHA MULENGYA

from a heart that knows how to say, "I am thankful." Gratitude helps you accept what you have and trust God for what you need. It teaches you to enjoy the present and stop worrying about the future. When you are grateful, you stop comparing and start celebrating. You stop complaining and start appreciating. You stop doubting and start believing. Contentment is not about having everything—it's about recognizing that God is enough. Gratitude reminds you that you are blessed, even in the middle of a storm. And when you live with contentment, you live with confidence. *"Godliness with contentment is great gain."* —1 Timothy 6:6

Calmness is the fruit of a thankful spirit. In a world full of noise, stress, and pressure, calmness is a rare treasure. Gratitude helps you slow down, breathe deeply, and rest in God's promises. It quiets your fears and calms your thoughts. It reminds you that God is in control, even when life feels out of control. When you are grateful, you stop panicking and start praying. You stop rushing and start resting. You stop reacting and start reflecting. Calmness is not weakness—it's wisdom. It's the ability to trust God even when things don't make sense. Gratitude helps you stay grounded, focused, and peaceful. And when you grow in calmness, you grow in strength. *"Be still, and know that I am God."* —Psalm 46:10

Celebration is the overflow of a grateful life. Gratitude turns ordinary moments into miracles. It helps you see beauty in the small things and joy in the journey. When you are thankful, every day becomes a reason to celebrate. You celebrate life, love, and the goodness of God. You celebrate progress, not just perfection. You celebrate people, not just possessions. Gratitude makes your heart sing and your soul dance. It fills your life with laughter, light, and love. Celebration is not just for special occasions—it's for every breath you take. When you grow with gratitude, you learn to rejoice always. And when you rejoice, you reflect the glory of God. *"Rejoice in the Lord always. I will say it again: Rejoice!"* —**Philippians 4:4**

Gratitude is a choice you make every day. It's not based on circumstances—it's based on conviction. You can choose to be grateful even when life is hard. You can choose to give thanks even when things don't go your way. Gratitude is a decision to trust God's goodness over your feelings. It's a declaration that God is faithful, no matter what. When you choose gratitude, you choose growth. You choose peace over panic. You choose worship over worry. You choose joy over jealousy. Gratitude is your daily victory. And every time you choose it, you become stronger. *"This is the day the Lord has made; let us rejoice and be glad in it."* —**Psalm 118:24**

Goodness grows where gratitude flows. When your heart is full of thanks, your life becomes full of grace. Gratitude helps you treat others with kindness, compassion, and love. It makes you more patient, more generous, and more forgiving. Goodness is not just about doing good—it's about being good. It's about letting God's character shine through you. Gratitude helps you become a better spouse, parent, friend, and leader. It helps you build stronger relationships and healthier communities. When you grow in gratitude, you grow in goodness. You become a light in the darkness and a voice of hope. You become a blessing to others. And your life becomes a testimony of God's love. *"Let your light shine before others, that they may see your good deeds and glorify your Father in heaven."* —**Matthew 5:16**

Gratitude transforms your perspective. It helps you see problems as possibilities. It helps you see pain as preparation. It helps you see delays as divine appointments. Gratitude gives you spiritual vision. It helps you look beyond the surface and see God's hand at work. It helps you trust the process and embrace the journey. When you are grateful, you stop asking "Why me?" and start saying "Thank You, Lord." You begin to see every moment as meaningful. You begin to see every challenge as a chance to grow. Gratitude changes how you think, how you speak, and how you live. And when your perspective changes, your life changes. *"Open my eyes that I may see wonderful things in your law."* —**Psalm 119:18**

Gratitude is the foundation of faith. It reminds you of what God has done and what He will do again. It helps you remember His promises and rely on His power. Gratitude strengthens your trust and deepens your devotion. It fuels your prayers and ignites your praise. When you are grateful, you believe that God is working— even when you don't see it. You believe that He is good—even when life is hard. You believe that He is near—even when you feel alone. Gratitude helps you walk by faith, not by sight. It helps you stand firm in storms and soar in seasons of success. And when your faith grows, your future glows. *"Now faith is confidence in what we hope for and assurance about what we do not see."* —**Hebrews 11:1**

Gratitude is contagious. When you live with a thankful heart, you inspire others to do the same. You become a source of encouragement, joy, and hope. Your words lift, your actions bless, and your presence heals. Gratitude spreads love, peace, and positivity. It creates a ripple effect that touches families, workplaces, and communities. When you grow with gratitude, you help others grow too. You become a leader of light and a messenger of mercy. You become a builder of bridges and a bringer of blessings. Gratitude is not just personal—it's powerful. And when you share it, you multiply it. *"Let us consider how we may spur one another on toward love and good deeds."* —**Hebrews 10:24**

SYAVIHA MULENGYA

This book is your invitation to grow. Grow in gratitude. Grow in goodness. Grow in grace. Let go of worry and embrace worship. Let go of fear and embrace faith. Let go of stress and embrace strength. Inside these pages, you'll find stories, scriptures, and steps to help you live a life of thankfulness. You'll discover how gratitude leads to contentment, calmness, and celebration. You'll learn how to rise above challenges and rejoice in every season. You'll be reminded that you are useful, valuable, and full of purpose. You'll see that there is hope for you—real, lasting, life-changing hope. So open your heart, turn the page, and let the journey begin. *"Enter His gates with thanksgiving and His courts with praise; give thanks to Him and praise His name."* **—Psalm 100:4.**

1

GRATEFUL LIFE IS A HAPPY LIFE

Gratitude is the gateway to joy. When you choose to be grateful, you unlock a deeper kind of happiness—one that doesn't depend on what you have, but on how you see. A grateful heart finds blessings in the ordinary and purpose even in pain. The Bible reminds us, *"This is the day the Lord has made; we will rejoice and be glad in it"* (**Psalm 118:24**). Gratitude helps you rejoice not because life is perfect, but because God is present. It shifts your focus from what's lacking to what's lasting. You begin to smile more, stress less, and see life through the lens of love. Gratitude doesn't erase your problems, but it gives you peace in the middle of them. It calms your spirit, lifts your mood, and strengthens your faith. A grateful life is a joyful life because it's rooted in trust, not trouble. It's not about pretending everything is fine—it's about praising God even when it's not. And that kind of joy is deep, durable, and divine. It cannot be stolen, shaken, or silenced.

SYAVIHA MULENGYA

Gratitude changes your attitude. Many people wait to be happy until everything goes right. But gratitude teaches you to be happy right now, even when things are not perfect. It's not about waiting for a better day—it's about worshiping in this one. The Apostle Paul said, *"In everything give thanks; for this is the will of God in Christ Jesus for you"* (**1 Thessalonians 5:18**). Gratitude is not just a reaction—it's a decision. It helps you stop comparing, complaining, and criticizing. Instead, you start celebrating, complimenting, and caring. Your words become sweeter, your thoughts become clearer, and your heart becomes lighter. Gratitude brings peace to your mind and purpose to your steps. It helps you walk with confidence, speak with kindness, and live with joy. When you live with a thankful heart, you carry heaven's hope into every room. And that hope is contagious—it lifts others, heals wounds, and builds bridges. Gratitude doesn't just change how you feel—it changes how you live.

Gratitude multiplies what matters. When you are grateful, you begin to see how much you already have. You realize that joy isn't found in getting more—it's found in appreciating what God has already given. You may not have everything you want, but you have more than enough to be thankful for. Gratitude opens your eyes to the gifts you've overlooked: breath in your lungs, love in your life, and grace for each day. Jesus said, *"I have come that they may have life, and have it to the full"* (**John 10:10**). A full life is not a life full of things—it's a life full of thanks. When you count your blessings, your burdens feel lighter. When you give thanks, your heart grows stronger. Gratitude doesn't just change your mood—it changes your movement. It moves you from bitterness to better, from pressure to peace, from stress to strength. It helps you walk in joy, live with purpose, and shine with hope. Truly, a grateful life is a happy life—because it's a life that sees God's hand in everything.

SYAVIHA MULENGYA

Did You Get the Gift?

Muyisa was a young man with big dreams. His birthday was coming, and he hoped his grandfather would send him a fantastic gift, like a sports car. He imagined driving the car and impressing his friends.

On his birthday, a package arrived from his grandfather. Muyisa opened it eagerly, expecting something amazing. But inside was a small, rusty box. He frowned and felt deeply disappointed. When he opened the box, he found an old, dusty piece of jewelry. He muttered angrily, *"What is this? I didn't want this!"* Upset, he tossed the box into a corner and forgot about it.

A few days later, another package arrived. It was a letter from his grandfather that read: *"Muyisa, did you get the gift I sent you? That gift is special. It will change your life."*

Muyisa didn't understand. He looked at the box again, but still thought, *"How can this useless thing change my life?"* Frustrated, he left it where it was.

One afternoon, his best friend, Muvuya, came to visit. He noticed the dusty box and asked, *"What's that?"*

Muyisa replied, annoyed, *"It's just some junk my grandfather sent me. I thought I'd get something good, like a car, but instead, I got this useless thing."*

Muvuya picked up the box and examined the jewelry. After a moment, he said, *"I don't know, Muyisa. This doesn't look like junk. Why don't you take it to a shop to check its value?"*

Muyisa rolled his eyes. *"What's the point? It's worth nothing. It's just a waste of time."*

SYAVIHA MULENGYA

Muvuya shook his head and insisted, *"Come on, Muyisa. You have nothing to lose. At least find out if it's worth something."*

After some convincing, Muyisa finally agreed. The next day, he and Muvuya went to a jewelry shop. The appraiser carefully examined the piece, and Muyisa waited without much hope. Then the appraiser said something that shocked them both: *"This is a rare antique. It's worth millions of dollars!"*

Muyisa couldn't believe it. *"Millions? Are you sure?"* he asked, his voice trembling. He had been struggling with money, and now, this forgotten gift was the answer to his problems.

With the money, Muyisa helped his family, started a small business, and even bought the sports car he had always wanted. But more importantly, he learned a valuable lesson. He realized his grandfather's gift wasn't just about the money. It was about teaching him to look beyond how things appear and to be grateful for the blessings in his life, even when they seem small or unimportant.

To show his gratitude, Muyisa organized a big celebration to honor his grandfather. He invited friends and family and told them the story of the gift. He also thanked Muvuya for persuading him to check the jewelry. The party was filled with joy, laughter, and heartfelt speeches, reminding everyone of the power of gratitude and hidden blessings.

The Hidden Key to Lasting Happiness

1. Satisfaction

Gratitude opens the door to lasting happiness by helping us truly appreciate what we already have. Instead of constantly longing for more, gratitude shifts our focus to the blessings surrounding us. By taking even a moment to thank God for His gifts, we begin to see how rich and fortunate we are. This thankfulness brings a deep sense of contentment, where we stop chasing after things we think we need and instead find joy in the present. Life's challenges may remain, but gratitude allows us to experience peace and happiness amidst them, teaching us that fulfillment often lies in simplicity and appreciation.

In **Philippians 4:11-12**, Paul writes, "I have learned to be content whatever the circumstances." These wise words remind us that joy is not dependent on external situations, but on our attitude of gratitude. Whether life is going well or feels overwhelming, being grateful helps us pause and cherish the small blessings that brighten each day. It could be the kindness of a loved one, the beauty of nature, or simply the gift of health. Gratitude redefines happiness, showing us that it doesn't come from having everything but from valuing what matters most.

When gratitude becomes part of our lives, we stop comparing ourselves to others. This liberates us from envy and feelings of inadequacy. Instead, we find strength in our personal journeys and begin to celebrate the unique paths we are walking. It helps us reflect on how far we've come, rather than obsessing over what we may lack. Gratitude allows us to appreciate the successes and blessings we've already received, making our lives feel more abundant and fulfilling.

Ultimately, the contentment that gratitude brings gives us peace of mind. It frees us from the pressures of keeping up with others or chasing unrealistic goals. This mental calmness makes life more meaningful as we learn to focus on what truly brings us joy and fulfillment. Gratitude transforms not just how we see the world but also how we live in it, creating an inner tranquility that leads to a richer, more joyful life.

2. Serenity

Gratitude is a key to finding peace and calm in our lives. It shifts our focus from anxiety to God's faithfulness and provision. When we practice gratitude, we learn to trust that God is always taking care of us, no matter the challenges we face. This trust creates a sense of serenity where we feel balanced and centered rather than overwhelmed by life's ups and downs. In John 14:27, Jesus gives us His promise: *"Peace I leave with you; my peace I give you."* Gratitude opens our hearts to receive this peace and allows it to flow through us. It reminds us that God's presence brings calmness, even in uncertain times.

Gratitude helps us to let go of the worries and fears that weigh us down. Instead of focusing on the negatives, it encourages us to appreciate the positive moments and blessings in our lives. This shift in perspective brings comfort and helps us to navigate difficult situations with confidence and hope. Gratitude is not about ignoring the problems we face—it's about facing them with a steady and clear mind. As we give thanks for God's blessings, we discover an unshakable calm that guides us through life's storms. In Philippians 4:6-7, it says, *"By prayer and petition, with thanksgiving, present your requests to God. And the peace of God, which transcends all understanding, will guard your hearts and your minds in Christ Jesus."*

Serenity through gratitude also empowers us to see solutions instead of dwelling on fears. A grateful heart enables us to trust in God's plan and believe that everything will work out for our good. This trust brings a sense of comfort and allows us to approach each day with hope. By focusing on God's blessings and grace, we can

SYAVIHA MULENGYA

remain calm even when facing challenges. Gratitude reminds us that His guidance and love are always with us, lighting our path and bringing us peace.

Practicing gratitude also strengthens our faith and deepens our relationship with God. When we thank Him for His blessings, we open our hearts to His presence and align ourselves with His will. Gratitude is a way of acknowledging His goodness and trusting in His purpose for our lives. As we express thankfulness, we grow closer to Him and find the calmness that comes from knowing He is in control. In Isaiah 26:3, it says, *"You will keep in perfect peace those whose minds are steadfast, because they trust in you."*

Gratitude inspires us to share peace and calmness with others. As we experience God's blessings, we are called to be a source of encouragement and positivity in the lives of those around us. By showing appreciation and kindness, we create an atmosphere of harmony and build stronger connections with others. Gratitude multiplies blessings and brings peace not only to our own hearts but also to our families, communities, and beyond. It reminds us that God's love and peace are meant to be shared, creating a ripple effect of goodness in the world. The gift of serenity is life-changing. It makes us healthier, happier, and better at making decisions. When we are calm, we build stronger relationships, achieve our goals with clarity, and enjoy the beauty of every moment. Gratitude is the key to unlocking this peaceful and balanced way of living.

3. Self-Esteem

Gratitude helps us understand our value and worth. By thanking God for creating us, we start to see how special and important we are. This feeling grows our self-esteem and makes us feel confident in who we are. Gratitude reminds us to appreciate our strengths, talents, and unique qualities, allowing us to live with pride and purpose.

Psalm 139:14 offers this powerful truth: *"I praise you because I am fearfully and wonderfully made."* These words remind us that we were created by God with care and love. Through gratitude, we begin to see ourselves as valuable and cherished. It helps us focus on our blessings and recognize how much we are capable of achieving.

With strong self-esteem, we are not afraid to take risks or embrace challenges. Gratitude builds confidence, showing us that we have the ability to overcome obstacles and reach our goals. It encourages us to believe in ourselves and trust God's purpose for our lives. Self-esteem also empowers us to lift others up. When we value ourselves, we are better able to share kindness and support with the people around us. Gratitude creates a cycle of positivity, where we recognize our own worth and inspire others to see theirs too, leading to happier and healthier relationships.

4. Sanity

Gratitude is a powerful tool for keeping our minds healthy and balanced. When we focus on being thankful, we push away negativity and fear. This clears our thoughts and helps us stay focused on what truly matters. Gratitude fills our minds with hope and positivity, protecting us from the stress and confusion that can take over during tough times.

Isaiah 26:3 gives us reassurance: *"You will keep in perfect peace those whose minds are steadfast, because they trust in you."* By trusting God and practicing gratitude, we can protect our mental health. A thankful mind is less likely to feel overwhelmed or distracted by unhelpful thoughts. Gratitude keeps us grounded, making it easier to stay calm and make excellent decisions. When our minds are balanced, we feel more in control of our emotions and actions. Gratitude helps us handle challenges with patience and wisdom. It gives us the mental strength to stay steady in the face of uncertainty and find joy even in hard times. Sanity means having a mind that is clear, calm, and focused. Gratitude protects this gift by reminding us of the blessings and support that surround us. It is the foundation of mental well-being and a healthier, more peaceful life.

5. Simplicity

Gratitude reminds us that happiness doesn't come from having more, but from appreciating the simple things we already have. A warm meal, the smile of a loved one, or the beauty of a sunrise can fill our hearts with joy when we choose to be grateful for them. By focusing on these small blessings, we learn to embrace a simpler and more meaningful life, free from the constant pressure to want more.

In **Matthew 6:25-26**, Jesus teaches us, *"Do not worry about your life, what you will eat or drink; or about your body, what you will wear."* This message encourages us to trust that God will provide for our needs. Gratitude helps us let go of unnecessary worries about material things and instead appreciate the everyday moments that bring joy and peace.

Living simply means we focus on what really matters, like spending time with loved ones, helping others, and enjoying the beauty of life. When we stop chasing after things we don't need, we free ourselves from stress and clutter. Gratitude helps us slow down and find joy in the present, making life feel less complicated and more fulfilling. Ultimately, simplicity brings freedom and peace. A grateful heart finds happiness in the little things, realizing that true wealth lies not in possessions but in the richness of relationships, experiences, and faith. By practicing gratitude, we can live a simpler, more joyful life.

6. Sleep

Gratitude has the power to calm our minds and improve our sleep. When we thank God for His blessings and protection at the end of the day, we feel safe and at peace. This sense of security relaxes our minds and bodies, making it easier to fall asleep and enjoy deep, restful sleep. Gratitude acts like a soothing blanket, wrapping us in comfort.

In **Psalm 4:8**, it says, *"In peace I will lie down and sleep, for you alone, Lord, make me dwell in safety."* These words remind us that God is watching over us, even as we sleep. By focusing on thankfulness instead of worries, we can let go of anxious thoughts that often keep us awake at night. Gratitude shifts our minds from fear to trust, helping us rest in peace.

Good sleep is vital for our health and well-being. It keeps our minds sharp, our emotions balanced, and our bodies strong. When we approach bedtime with gratitude, we create a peaceful routine that prepares us for a good night's rest. Simple acts like thanking God for the day's blessings can make a big difference.

By improving our sleep, gratitude also improves our energy, mood, and overall health. A well-rested person can face the day with more positivity and strength. Gratitude is a gift that doesn't just brighten our days but also brings calm to our nights.

7. Strength

Gratitude gives us the strength to face life's challenges. When we focus on the blessings God has given us, we feel joy and hope.

This joy becomes a source of inner strength, helping us overcome difficulties with courage and confidence. Gratitude empowers us to trust in God's plan, even when life feels hard.

In **Nehemiah 8:10**, it says, *"The joy of the Lord is your strength."* These words remind us that joy and gratitude go hand in hand. When we are thankful, we find reasons to keep going, even in tough times. Gratitude helps us shift our perspective from problems to possibilities, making us resilient.

Strength doesn't just mean physical power—it's also about emotional and spiritual resilience. Gratitude builds this resilience by reminding us of the support, love, and blessings that surround us. It gives us confidence to face challenges, knowing we are never alone.

A thankful heart draws strength not only from God but also from the people who care for us. Gratitude brings us closer to others, creating a support system that lifts us up during tough times. It helps us face life with courage, determination, and trust in God's goodness.

8. Stress Relief

Gratitude is a natural remedy for stress. When we thank God for His blessings, it shifts our focus from worries to trust. Gratitude reminds us that we are not alone in our struggles and that God is always in control. This trust eases our fears and helps us stay calm, even in difficult situations. In **Philippians 4:6-7**, it says, *"Do not be anxious about anything, but in every situation, by prayer and petition, with thanksgiving, present your requests to God."* By practicing gratitude and turning to prayer, we invite God's peace into our lives. This peace acts as a shield, protecting us from overwhelming stress and anxiety.

SYAVIHA MULENGYA

Reducing stress allows us to live healthier and happier lives. Gratitude clears our minds and helps us focus on the positive, making it easier to tackle challenges with a clear head. It also improves our relationships, as a calm and thankful attitude makes us more patient and kind to others.

Gratitude creates a sense of balance, reminding us to breathe, trust, and let go of what we can't control. It allows us to enjoy life more fully, free from the weight of constant worry. By practicing gratitude daily, we can experience a more peaceful and stress-free life.

2

THE GOOD LIFE

1. Enhance

Gratitude has the power to make our lives better in many ways. When we focus on the things we are thankful for, we feel happier and more content. It shifts our minds from what we don't have to what we do have, making us more positive and joyful. This change in perspective helps us appreciate the blessings in our lives, no matter how big or small they may be. Gratitude enhances our overall sense of happiness and well-being.

In **1 Thessalonians 5:18**, the Bible tells us, *"Give thanks in all circumstances; for this is God's will for you in Christ Jesus."* These words remind us that gratitude should be part of our daily lives. By practicing it every day, we become more satisfied and find joy even in challenging situations. Gratitude lifts our spirits and helps us see life from a more positive angle.

Gratitude also makes our relationships stronger. When we thank others for their kindness or support, we show them how much they mean to us. This strengthens the bond between us and

SYAVIHA MULENGYA

brings joy to both sides. **Proverbs 17:22** says, *"A cheerful heart is good medicine, but a crushed spirit dries up the bones."* Gratitude fills our hearts with cheerfulness, making our interactions with others more meaningful and loving.

When gratitude becomes a habit, it enhances every aspect of our lives. It brings joy, peace, and fulfillment while teaching us to celebrate the blessings we receive each day. Gratitude is a simple yet powerful way to improve our mood, relationships, and overall happiness.

2. Elevate Our Mood

Gratitude is a powerful tool that lifts our spirits and makes us happy. When we focus on the good things in our lives, our mood improves and we feel lighter. Even during tough times, gratitude helps us see the bright side and find reasons to smile. It reminds us that there is always something to be thankful for, no matter the challenges we face.

Philippians 4:4 encourages us to rejoice: *"Rejoice in the Lord always. I will say it again: Rejoice!"* Gratitude helps us follow this advice by keeping our minds focused on the positives in life. It makes us more optimistic and helps us stay hopeful, even when things seem difficult. Gratitude acts as a source of light that brightens our days and keeps negativity away.

When our mood is positive, it becomes easier to handle problems and enjoy life's moments. Gratitude helps us maintain this positive mindset, making us more resilient and joyful. **Psalm 118:24** reminds us to celebrate each day: *"This is the day that the Lord has made; let us rejoice and be glad in it."* Gratitude helps us embrace the gift of every day with gladness and appreciation.

By elevating our mood, gratitude also improves our relationships and decision-making. A joyful heart spreads positivity to those around us, making the world feel kinder and brighter. Gratitude is a simple way to create happiness within ourselves and share it with others.

3. Encourage

Gratitude inspires us to think positively and stay hopeful. It shifts our focus from negative thoughts to positive ones, making it easier to see the good in every situation. When we are thankful, we train our minds to focus on blessings rather than worries. This mindset helps us stay optimistic and face life's challenges with confidence.

In **Philippians 4:8**, we are reminded to think about positive things: *"Whatever is true, whatever is noble, whatever is right, whatever is pure, whatever is lovely, whatever is admirable—if anything is excellent or praiseworthy—think about such things."* Gratitude helps us follow this advice by encouraging us to look for the good in our lives. It helps us appreciate beauty, kindness, and love, even when times are tough.

Positive thinking is important because it helps us stay strong and hopeful during difficult moments. Gratitude gives us the courage to keep going and the belief that things will get better. **Romans 12:12** encourages us to be joyful, patient, and faithful: *"Be joyful in hope, patient in affliction, faithful in prayer."* Gratitude helps us live out these values by giving us strength and optimism.

By practicing gratitude every day, we create a habit of positive thinking. This encourages us to trust in God's plan and recognize the blessings that surround us. Gratitude is a gentle reminder to stay hopeful, no matter what life brings our way.

SYAVIHA MULENGYA

4. Empower

Gratitude has the ability to make us feel strong and confident. When we take time to be thankful, we recognize the blessings and support in our lives. This builds courage and reminds us that we are not alone. Gratitude gives us the strength to handle life's challenges with confidence and trust.

In **Nehemiah 8:10**, it says, *"The joy of the Lord is your strength."* Gratitude helps us feel this joy and draw strength from God's blessings. By focusing on what we are thankful for, we find hope and resilience in tough times. Gratitude empowers us to believe in ourselves and face obstacles with courage. Feeling empowered means knowing we can overcome difficulties and achieve our goals. Gratitude plays a key role in this by reminding us of our abilities and the love and support around us. **Isaiah 40:31** offers encouragement: *"But those who hope in the Lord will renew their strength. They will soar on wings like eagles; they will run and not grow weary, they will walk and not be faint."* Gratitude helps us renew our strength and soar through life's challenges.

By empowering us, gratitude improves our relationships, decisions, and overall outlook. It reminds us to stay strong and trust in God's plan, even when life feels uncertain. Gratitude is a source of courage and hope that helps us grow into better, stronger individuals.

5. Enrich Our Lives

Gratitude has the power to make life richer and more meaningful. When we are thankful, we notice and appreciate the beauty and blessings that surround us. Gratitude opens our eyes to the small, everyday joys we often overlook—a loving smile, a kind gesture, or the vibrant colors of nature. This appreciation deepens our connection to the world around us, making our lives feel fuller and more rewarding.

In **Psalm 103:2,** we are reminded, *"Praise the Lord, my soul, and forget not all his benefits."* Gratitude helps us remember and cherish these blessings. It shifts our attention away from what we think is missing in our lives and toward the abundance we already have. This mindset enriches our experiences, allowing us to feel happier and more fulfilled in our daily lives.

An enriched life is filled with love, joy, and meaningful relationships. Gratitude helps us value the people and moments that matter most. When we practice thankfulness, we strengthen our connections with family and friends, creating deeper bonds built on appreciation and kindness. **James 1:17** tells us, *"Every good and perfect gift is from above."* Gratitude helps us recognize these gifts from God and treasure them.

By enriching our lives, gratitude also inspires us to give back. When we are aware of the blessings we have received, we are more likely to share them with others, spreading love and kindness. This creates a cycle of generosity and thankfulness, where our lives become even richer through the joy of giving and receiving.

6. Ease Stress

Gratitude is a natural antidote to stress and anxiety. When we focus on the things we are thankful for, it calms our minds and reduces our worries. Gratitude shifts our attention from problems to blessings, helping us find peace even in difficult situations. This sense of peace allows us to manage stress more effectively, staying grounded and relaxed.

In **Philippians 4:6-7,** it says, *"Do not be anxious about anything, but in every situation, by prayer and petition, with thanksgiving,* *present your requests to God. And the peace of God, which transcends all understanding, will guard your hearts and your minds in Christ Jesus."* Gratitude brings this peace into our lives, making us feel safe and cared for. It reminds us to trust in God and let go of worries we cannot control.

A life with less stress is a life with more happiness and freedom. Gratitude helps us focus on the present moment instead of dwelling on the past or fearing the future. **Matthew 6:34** encourages us, *"Do not worry about tomorrow, for tomorrow will worry about itself."* By practicing gratitude, we learn to appreciate each day and face challenges with a calm and steady mind.

Over time, gratitude fosters a more peaceful, balanced way of living. It teaches us to focus on what truly matters and let go of unnecessary fears. By easing stress, gratitude allows us to enjoy life more fully, creating a sense of joy and calm in our everyday experiences.

7. Enjoy Every Moment

Gratitude helps us slow down and savor life's precious moments. When we are thankful, we become more present and mindful, appreciating the here and now. Instead of rushing through life, we take time to enjoy its simple pleasures—a shared laugh, a warm meal, or a quiet moment of reflection. Gratitude turns ordinary moments into extraordinary ones, filling our days with joy.

Psalm 118:24 reminds us, *"This is the day that the Lord has made; let us rejoice and be glad in it."* Gratitude encourages us to rejoice in each day, treating it as a gift from God. By focusing on the present, we find happiness in the little things, turning even small joys into meaningful memories. This practice of thankfulness makes each day more special.

Living in the moment helps us find peace and satisfaction. Gratitude prevents us from dwelling on the past or worrying about the future, keeping us grounded in the present. **Ecclesiastes 3:12-13** tells us, *"There is nothing better for people than to be happy and to do good while they live."* Gratitude helps us live this way, finding satisfaction in our daily lives and spreading joy to those around us.

By helping us enjoy every moment, gratitude makes life more vibrant and fulfilling. It teaches us to value each experience and treasure every blessing, no matter how small. Gratitude transforms the way we see the world, making every moment a chance to feel joy and appreciation.

8. Expand Our Perspective

Gratitude helps us see beyond our immediate circumstances, offering a broader, more hopeful perspective on life. When we are thankful, we recognize that even difficult times can bring blessings. Gratitude reminds us that challenges often lead to growth, teaching us valuable lessons and strengthening our faith. This expanded perspective helps us stay positive and trust that everything happens for a reason.

In **Romans 8:28**, it says, *"And we know that in all things God works for the good of those who love him."* Gratitude helps us believe in this promise, even when life feels uncertain. It encourages us to look for the silver lining in every situation, trusting that God's plan is always for our good. This broader perspective allows us to face challenges with courage and hope.

Gratitude also helps us appreciate the interconnectedness of our lives. It shows us how our actions and blessings affect others, inspiring us to be more compassionate and generous. **Proverbs 3:5-6** encourages us to trust in God's plan: *"Trust in the Lord with all* *your heart and lean not on your own understanding; in all your ways submit to him, and he will make your paths straight."* Gratitude strengthens this trust, helping us see the bigger picture.

By expanding our perspective, gratitude transforms the way we approach life. It helps us find purpose and meaning in every experience, leading to greater happiness and fulfillment. Gratitude reminds us that no matter what happens, we are surrounded by blessings and opportunities.

Gratitude is What You Need

Gratitude is a powerful force that can change the way we see the world. It helps us discover the beauty and blessings that are already present in our lives. Often, happiness feels far away, but gratitude shows us that the solution to our joy is closer than we think. By appreciating what we have, who we are, and what we've been given, life becomes more meaningful. Gratitude allows us to experience a life filled with beauty, peace, and abundance, as it shifts our focus from what we lack to all that we already have.

One of the most profound benefits of gratitude is the ability to see our blessings clearly. So often, we focus on what is missing in our lives—on the things we want but don't have. This focus blinds us to the incredible gifts we've been given. Gratitude helps us turn our attention to what truly matters. It enables us to recognize small yet significant blessings, like the warmth of the sun on our skin, the laughter of a friend, or the comfort of a meal shared with loved ones. As we develop an attitude of gratitude, we realize how much we truly have, and life feels richer and more joyful.

Another way gratitude transforms us is by helping us discover our inner beauty. In today's world, where social media often sets impossible standards for appearance and success, it's easy to feel like we're not enough. We might criticize ourselves for not looking a certain way or achieving what others have. However, gratitude changes this perspective. It allows us to appreciate our unique qualities and understand that true beauty comes from within. Gratitude reminds us that our worth is not determined by external standards but by the love, kindness, and strength we bring to the world.

Furthermore, gratitude reveals the priceless value of non-material things. In our pursuit of happiness, we often believe that material possessions will bring us joy. We chase after the latest gadgets, expensive clothes, or luxurious lifestyles, hoping they'll make us feel fulfilled. But gratitude shows us that true happiness comes from intangible things: love, relationships, and meaningful experiences. It teaches us that the things we thought we lacked often pale in comparison to the love and support we already have in our lives. A simple hug, a heartfelt conversation, or a moment of quiet reflection can bring more happiness than any material possession.

An inspiring story illustrates how gratitude can bring clarity and transform our lives. A woman felt unhappy in her marriage because her husband didn't take her out often. Believing she deserved better, she filed for divorce. However, after hearing others share their struggles in relationships, she realized how minor her concerns were. Her husband was caring, supportive, and loyal — qualities she had overlooked. Gratitude helped her recognize the goodness in her relationship and see her husband's true value. This realization changed her perspective, and she chose to focus on the blessings in her marriage rather than the small things she felt were missing.

SYAVIHA MULENGYA

Gratitude is a life-changing practice that leads to a great life. It opens our eyes to the blessings that surround us and fills our hearts with peace and joy. By appreciating what we have and who we are, we can create a life that feels rich in love, beauty, and meaning. Gratitude shifts our focus from what we lack to the abundance already present, proving that happiness has always been within our reach. Embracing gratitude is not just a choice—it is the foundation of a fulfilling and joyful life.

3

IT'S NOT LITTLE,
IT'S A LOT.

Sometimes we look at our lives and feel like we don't have enough. We compare ourselves to others and think we are behind, lacking, or forgotten. But the truth is, God has already given us more than we realize. The breath in your lungs, the strength in your spirit, the love in your heart—these are not small things. They are signs of His goodness and grace. The Bible says, *"Do not despise these small beginnings, for the Lord rejoices to see the work begin"* (**Zechariah 4:10**). What looks small to man is big in God's hands. Your gifts, your story, your journey—they matter. You are not empty; you are equipped. You are not overlooked; you are overflowing. When you count what you have, you'll see that it's not little—it's a lot.

God multiplies what you honor. When you thank God for what's in your hand, He blesses it beyond measure. The boy with five loaves and two fish didn't have much—but when he gave it to Jesus, it fed thousands. The widow with a little oil saw it multiply when she obeyed the Word. The Bible says, *"Whoever can be*
SYAVIHA MULENGYA

trusted with very little can also be trusted with much" (**Luke 16:10**). Gratitude opens your eyes to abundance. Faith opens your hands to receive more. What you have may seem small, but in God's eyes, it's a seed for something great. Don't say, "It's just a little"—say, "It's already a lot." Because with God, little becomes plenty, and enough becomes overflow. You are not lacking—you are loaded with purpose, potential, and power.

More Than Enough

Gratitude is one of the simplest yet most impactful practices that can transform how we view life. It allows us to find joy and meaning in the little things that often go unnoticed, showing us that happiness doesn't depend on grand gestures or material wealth. A beautiful story perfectly illustrates this point.

A man once visited a thrift store and bought a small toy car for his son. When the boy received the gift, he was so overwhelmed with happiness that he hugged his father and mother tightly and shared his excitement with them. When his brother came home, the boy eagerly told him about the amazing gift his father had given him. His joy didn't stop there—he called his uncles and everyone he knew to share his excitement about the toy car. The father was deeply moved by how much happiness the simple gift brought his son. Seeing his son's passion, the father continued buying toy cars. Over time, the boy's love for cars grew, and he eventually became a skilled mechanic and successful car dealer, all starting from that one small toy car.

This story highlights how gratitude for small blessings can lead to big changes. The boy's love for cars and his eventual career stemmed from his genuine appreciation for the toy car. Gratitude opened his eyes to his passion, shaping his future in ways he never imagined. By practicing gratitude, we can uncover hidden blessings in our lives and discover new paths that bring us joy and fulfillment.

Gratitude is a remarkable gift that allows us to find joy in the smallest moments, unlocking a sense of happiness and peace that transforms our lives. Sometimes, the tiniest gestures hold the most meaning, showing us that true fulfillment doesn't come from big, flashy things but from the thoughtfulness and love behind them.

Take the example of the boy who received a toy car from his father. It was an ordinary gift, nothing lavish, at first sight. Yet, the boy's pure excitement and gratitude for the toy car turned it into something extraordinary. He hugged his mother, told his brother, and even called his uncles, spreading his joy to everyone around him. This simple act of gratitude touched his father's heart so deeply that he continued buying toy cars for his son, supporting his newfound passion. Over time, the boy's love for cars flourished— he became an excellent mechanic and later a successful car dealer. What started as a small toy blossomed into a career and purpose, all because of the boy's gratitude.

Gratitude teaches us to recognize the blessings that often go unnoticed. The boy didn't just see a toy car; he saw a meaningful gift that sparked his passion. In life, we often overlook the blessings we already have, focusing instead on what we lack. Practicing gratitude helps us shift our perspective, allowing us to appreciate the small moments that bring joy and meaning. Whether it's the warmth of sunshine, the laughter of loved ones, or a simple act of kindness, gratitude helps us find value in the ordinary.

Beyond blessings, gratitude also reveals our inner beauty. The boy's enthusiasm and genuine appreciation showcased his pure and joyful spirit, touching the hearts of those around him. Gratitude helps us see the positive qualities within ourselves—

SYAVIHA MULENGYA

qualities like kindness, love, and generosity—that make us unique. It encourages us to embrace who we are and share our best selves with the world.

Moreover, gratitude shifts our focus from material possessions to deeper connections and experiences. The boy's happiness didn't come from the price of the toy car; it came from the love and thoughtfulness behind the gift. Gratitude teaches us to value relationships, shared moments, and the intangible joys of life. By doing so, it strengthens our bonds with others, fostering love and connection that enrich our lives.

Finally, gratitude helps us discover our purpose. For the boy, his gratitude for the toy car revealed his love for cars, guiding him toward a fulfilling career. When we practice gratitude, we become more aware of what makes us happy and passionate, leading us to our true calling. Gratitude serves as a compass, pointing us toward the things that bring meaning to our lives.

In the end, gratitude is about finding joy and purpose in the little things. It's the small moments—like a toy car or a kind word—that have the power to create big changes. By embracing gratitude, we can unlock happiness, strengthen our relationships, and discover a life full of blessings, beauty, and meaning. The simplest acts of appreciation can have the most profound impact, reminding us that life's greatest treasures are often hidden in plain sight.

1. Worth: Recognizing Our True Value

Gratitude helps us see the worth God has placed in each of us. When we take time to thank God for our unique qualities, we begin to recognize how fearfully and wonderfully we are made. **Psalm 139:14** tells us, *"I praise you because I am fearfully and wonderfully made; your works are wonderful, I know that full well."* Gratitude teaches us to appreciate the talents, abilities, and strengths God has given us.

By focusing on these blessings, we realize that our value isn't determined by the world's standards, but by God's plan for us. When we practice gratitude, we acknowledge the role we play in His creation. **Ephesians 2:10** reminds us, *"For we are God's handiwork, created in Christ Jesus to do good works, which God prepared in advance for us to do."* Recognizing our worth encourages us to embrace our purpose and live with confidence, knowing we have been made uniquely for great things.

2. Wealth: Finding Riches in God's Blessings

True wealth goes far beyond the money we earn or the possessions we accumulate. It lies in the love we share, the relationships we nurture, and the blessings God has poured into our lives. Gratitude is the key that opens our eyes to this abundance, helping us realize that we are already rich in what truly matters. **Proverbs 10:22** reminds us, *"The blessing of the Lord brings wealth, without painful toil for it."* This scripture teaches us that God's blessings do not come with stress or exhaustion, but with peace and fulfillment.

When we practice gratitude, we become aware of the gifts we often take for granted. The joy of spending time with loved ones, the blessing of good health, and the comfort of a kind word—these are treasures that cannot be measured in earthly terms. By thanking God for these gifts, we experience a sense of richness that no amount of money can replicate. Gratitude transforms our perspective, showing us that even in moments of difficulty, we are surrounded by God's goodness and love.

SYAVIHA MULENGYA

Gratitude also helps us shift our focus from material wealth to spiritual abundance. In **Matthew 6:19-20**, Jesus urges us, *"Do not store up for yourselves treasures on earth, where moths and vermin destroy, and where thieves break in and steal. But store up for yourselves treasures in heaven."* This passage reminds us that earthly possessions are temporary, but the love, joy, and peace we cultivate through a relationship with God are eternal. Gratitude directs our hearts toward these lasting treasures, allowing us to prioritize what truly matters.

Moreover, a grateful heart helps us enjoy life's enduring riches. When we focus on what God has given us—His unconditional love, His promises, and the people He has placed in our lives—we find contentment. We no longer feel the need to chase after temporary pleasures or compare our lives to others. Gratitude replaces envy with joy and worry with trust. It allows us to live with a deep sense of satisfaction, knowing that we are cared for by a loving Father who provides all we need.

3. Work: Discovering Our Mission Through Gratitude

Gratitude reveals the talents and passions God has placed within us, helping us discover our purpose. When we thank God for the skills we possess, we start to see how we can use them to glorify Him and help others. **Colossians 3:23** reminds us, *"Whatever you do, work at it with all your heart, as working for the Lord, not for human masters."* Gratitude allows us to find joy in serving and fulfilling the mission God has given us.

Through gratitude, we understand that our work is more than a job—it's a calling. Whether it's helping, creating, leading, or caring, God has equipped each of us uniquely. **Romans 12:6-8** reminds us of these gifts: *"We have different gifts, according to the grace given to each of us."* Recognizing our talents helps us align

SYAVIHA MULENGYA

our work with God's plan, giving us a sense of fulfillment and meaning.

4. Wonder: Seeing God's Glory in Everyday Life

Gratitude helps us see the wonder of God's creation in even the smallest details of life. When we thank God for a beautiful sunset, a kind word, or the laughter of loved ones, we begin to marvel at the miracles He places in our path daily. **Psalm 19:1** declares, *"The heavens declare the glory of God; the skies proclaim the work of his hands."* Gratitude opens our eyes to the magnificence of His handiwork.

This sense of wonder brings joy and amazement to our hearts, making each moment feel special. Gratitude reminds us that there is beauty and purpose in everything around us, whether grand or simple. **Ecclesiastes 3:11** teaches, *"He has made everything beautiful in its time."* By practicing gratitude, we grow closer to God and appreciate the wonders of His creation more fully.

5. Well-Being: Cherishing the Gift of Health

Gratitude encourages us to appreciate the health and happiness God has blessed us with. When we thank Him for our physical and mental well-being, we are inspired to take better care of ourselves. 1 **Corinthians 6:19-20** says, *"Do you not know that your bodies are temples of the Holy Spirit... Therefore honor God with your bodies."* Gratitude motivates us to treat our bodies with care and respect, recognizing them as gifts from Him.

Focusing on our health through gratitude also strengthens our spiritual well-being. **Philippians 4:6-7** reassures us, *"Do not be anxious about anything, but in every situation, by prayer and petition, with thanksgiving, present your requests to God. And the peace of God, which transcends all understanding, will guard your* *hearts and your minds in Christ Jesus."* Gratitude invites peace into our lives, fostering emotional balance and resilience.

6. Winning: Celebrating Progress Through Gratitude

Gratitude transforms our understanding of success by teaching us to celebrate progress rather than perfection. When we thank God for every step forward, we recognize that victory isn't just about achieving big goals—it's about growing in faith and character. **1 Corinthians 15:57** says, *"But thanks be to God! He gives us the victory through our Lord Jesus Christ."* Gratitude allows us to celebrate these everyday victories as gifts from Him.

By focusing on our journey rather than the destination, gratitude helps us find meaning in the process. **James 1:2-4** encourages us, *"Consider it pure joy, my brothers and sisters, whenever you face trials of many kinds... so that you may be mature and complete, not lacking anything."* Gratitude helps us see challenges as opportunities for growth, making every effort feel worthwhile.

7. Way: Trusting God's Path Through Gratitude

Gratitude guides us to trust in the path God has set before us. When we thank Him for the people, lessons, and blessings in our lives, we see His hand leading us toward our purpose. **Proverbs 3:5-6** encourages, *"Trust in the Lord with all your heart and lean not on your own understanding; in all your ways submit to him, and he will make your paths straight."* Gratitude strengthens our faith in His plan, even when the road ahead seems unclear.

By practicing gratitude, we come to recognize God's guidance in our lives. **Jeremiah 29:11** reassures us, *"For I know the plans I have for you,"* declares the Lord, *"plans to prosper you and not to harm you, plans to give you hope and a future."* Gratitude helps us trust that He is leading us toward greatness, giving us hope and confidence for the journey ahead.

4

WHEN WE FORGET TO BE THANKFUL

Malalamiko had a habit that defined his life—he complained about everything. No matter how good things were, he always found something wrong. He had a kind and caring wife, Maria, who worked hard to make him happy. But instead of appreciating her efforts, Malalamiko would grumble about her cooking, her cleaning, or her dress. "Why is this food not as tasty as it should be? Why haven't you cleaned this spot properly?" he would say. Maria felt heartbroken and unappreciated, and one day she packed her things and left. Malalamiko, still filled with complaints, believed it was her fault and decided to file for divorce.

At work, Malalamiko's constant complaining was no better. He had a good job that paid well, but he didn't see it as a blessing. He grumbled about his workload, his boss, and even his coworkers. "Why am I the only one doing all the hard work? Why can't they be more organized?" he would say. His negative attitude created tension in the office, and soon his boss had had enough.
SYAVIHA MULENGYA

Malalamiko was fired for his complaints, which caused problems in the workplace.

His habit of complaining followed him everywhere. One day, Malalamiko went to a store to buy groceries. The cashier, a young woman new to the job, was a bit slow to scan his items. Instead of being patient, Malalamiko raised his voice and yelled at her for wasting his time. "Why are you so slow? Can't you do anything right?" he shouted. The poor cashier burst into tears, and the store manager had to intervene. "Mr. Malalamiko," the manager said, "this behavior is unacceptable. Please leave our store." Humiliated, Malalamiko stormed out, still blaming the cashier for what had happened.

That night, as Malalamiko sat alone in his apartment, he began complaining again. He was unhappy with the noisy neighbors and the size of his apartment. He called his landlord to complain once more, but this time the landlord had reached his limit. "Mr. Malalamiko," the landlord said, "I can't deal with your constant complaints anymore. I'm breaking your lease. You'll need to find somewhere else to live." Now homeless and jobless, Malalamiko felt his life falling apart, but he still refused to see his role in the situation.

Desperate for answers, Malalamiko visited a counselor. He sat in the office and began listing all the things wrong with his life. "Why does everyone have a problem with me? Why can't people just do things right?" he said. The counselor listened carefully and then asked, "Mr. Malalamiko, do you know what your name means?" Surprised by the question, he replied, "My name? It means 'complainer.' Why does that matter?" The counselor smiled gently and said, "It matters because your name reflects how you've been living your life. Complaining has become your identity, and it's driving people away. You need to let go of this habit and start looking for what's good in your life."

The words struck a chord in Malalamiko. For the first time, he realized that the problem wasn't everyone else—it was his own attitude. The counselor encouraged him to practice gratitude. "Every day, write down three things you're thankful for," the counselor said. "Start small, and over time, you'll see how your life begins to change."

Determined to turn his life around, Malalamiko took the counselor's advice. He began focusing on the good things in his life rather than the bad. He wrote down simple blessings, like having food to eat, the warmth of the sun, or a kind word from a stranger. Slowly, his attitude began to change. He even changed his name to Baraka, meaning "blessing," as a way of embracing his new outlook on life.

Baraka reached out to Maria and apologized for how he had treated her. Moved by his sincerity and his changed attitude, Maria gave him a second chance. They remarried and built a happy, loving home together. Baraka also found a new job where his positive attitude made him a joy to be around. For the first time, he began to appreciate life and enjoy the people, places, and moments that once annoyed him.

The story of Mr. Malalamiko shows how complaining can destroy relationships, opportunities, and happiness. But it also shows the power of gratitude to transform a life. As the Bible teaches in **Philippians 2:14-15**, *"Do everything without grumbling or arguing, so that you may become blameless and pure, children of God without fault in a warped and crooked generation."* Gratitude opens our hearts to blessings, while complaining closes us off to the joy and peace that God wants for us. Let us choose gratitude and discover the fullness of life.

Losing Sight of What We Have

1. Sadness: Finding Joy Through Gratitude

When we are ungrateful, sadness can take over because we focus on what we don't have rather than appreciating what we do have. This negative outlook blinds us to the beauty and blessings around us. Constantly thinking about our shortcomings makes it hard to find joy in the small, everyday moments that can bring happiness. As the saying goes, *"Gratitude turns what we have into enough."*

Gratitude is like a light that brightens even the darkest times. By taking a moment to be thankful for life's simple gifts—a smile, a sunny day, or a meal—we can lift our spirits and find happiness in these little treasures. True joy isn't about having everything we want; it's about loving and valuing what we already have. As the saying reminds us, *"Happiness is not about getting what you want all the time. It's about loving what you have."*

When we practice gratitude, it shifts our thoughts from what's missing to what's already there. It changes how we see our lives, bringing in more contentment and peace. Focusing on blessings instead of problems helps us find joy every day. Gratitude has the power to replace sadness with happiness.

2. Selfishness: Learning Generosity Through Gratitude

Ungratefulness can make us selfish because it draws our attention to our own needs and desires. When we don't take the time to appreciate what we already have, we feel like it's never enough. This constant craving for more can lead us to put our wants above others' needs, making us less considerate. As the quote says, *"The more grateful you are, the more present you become."*

Gratitude changes this by helping us see the efforts and kindness of others. It reminds us to appreciate what people do for us and to acknowledge their contributions. By being thankful, we naturally become more compassionate and generous. Gratitude blooms in the soul, as beautifully described by the words, *"Gratitude is the fairest blossom which springs from the soul."*

When we let gratitude into our hearts, it opens a path to empathy. We begin to understand and care for others more deeply, and this fosters kindness and generosity. Instead of selfishly seeking more, gratitude encourages us to give back and share our blessings. Gratitude leads to a more loving and fulfilling way of life.

3. Strained Relationships: Building Bonds With Gratitude

Ungratefulness can harm relationships in ways we often overlook. When we fail to appreciate the people who care for us, they may feel unimportant or invisible. Imagine wrapping a beautiful gift for someone and never actually giving it to them—that's what it feels like when we feel gratitude but don't express it. As the saying goes, "Feeling gratitude and not expressing it is like wrapping a present and not giving it." Neglecting to show appreciation makes others feel taken for granted, and over time, this can weaken even the strongest bonds.

Gratitude, on the other hand, has the power to strengthen relationships. A simple "thank you" can brighten someone's day and make them feel valued. Expressing gratitude reminds others that their actions matter and are noticed. This act of appreciation creates a positive atmosphere in relationships, building trust, kindness, and deeper connections. As it's beautifully said,

"Gratitude is the memory of the heart." When we cherish and acknowledge the people in our lives, we bring them closer to us.

Practicing gratitude also helps us focus on the love and support we receive rather than the shortcomings we might notice in others. By being thankful for the efforts and care people show us, we nurture healthier, happier relationships. Gratitude fosters respect, joy, and understanding, creating a strong foundation for lasting connections. It helps us shift our attention from complaints to compliments, which can transform how we interact with loved ones.

Gratitude isn't just an emotion—it's an action. It's not enough to feel thankful; we must show it in words and deeds. Whether through kind words, small gestures, or simply spending quality time with someone, gratitude helps us grow closer to those who matter most. By choosing to express gratitude regularly, we can make our relationships more meaningful and fulfilling, bringing joy to both ourselves and the people we care about

4. Stagnation: Finding Growth Through Gratitude

Ungratefulness can keep us stuck, unable to grow or move forward. When we focus on what's missing, we feel trapped in negativity and fail to see the opportunities around us. Gratitude, however, unlocks potential. As the saying goes, *"Gratitude unlocks the fullness of life."*

Gratitude helps us look at situations differently, revealing possibilities we might have missed. It motivates us to celebrate progress, no matter how small, and to keep striving for improvement. As a reminder of gratitude's power, consider this: *"Gratitude makes sense of our past, brings peace for today, and creates a vision for tomorrow."*

SYAVIHA MULENGYA

When we are thankful for where we are and what we've achieved, it inspires us to pursue growth and goals. Gratitude creates a mindset that sees challenges as stepping stones rather than obstacles, propelling us toward a brighter future.

5. Short-Sightedness: Seeing the Bigger Picture Through Gratitude

Ungratefulness narrows our perspective, making us focus only on immediate struggles. This short-sighted view prevents us from seeing the bigger picture of life and its blessings. As the saying reminds us, *"Gratitude turns what we have into enough."*

Gratitude gives us a wider lens, allowing us to see how today's efforts shape tomorrow's outcomes. By being thankful for each step of the journey, we gain a deeper appreciation for life's process. As another quote puts it, *"Gratitude is not only the greatest of virtues but the parent of all others."*

With gratitude, we become more aware of the positives that surround us and the progress we've made. It helps us stay hopeful and focused, even during tough times. Gratitude opens our eyes to possibilities and strengthens our faith in the future.

6. Sour Attitude: Finding Positivity Through Gratitude

Ungratefulness often gives rise to a sour attitude, where we focus only on the negatives in life. This constant cycle of complaining and criticism can create a heavy atmosphere filled with gloom and hostility. When we always search for faults instead of blessings, we not only harm our own mental health but also affect the people around us. As the saying goes, "A grateful heart is a magnet for miracles."

Gratitude changes everything. It shifts our attention away from what's wrong and helps us see what's right. By taking a moment each day to appreciate life's blessings, even the smallest ones, we can cultivate a positive outlook. Gratitude reminds us that what we already have is enough—and often more than enough. It brings joy and contentment into our hearts, turning complaints into compliments and criticism into celebration.

When we practice gratitude, it's not just our mood that improves—our attitude brightens as well. We become more optimistic, cheerful, and open to life's possibilities. This positivity is contagious, spreading to those around us. Gratitude has the power to uplift not just ourselves, but also the people we interact with daily. A simple "thank you" or a word of appreciation can make a big difference in creating harmony and warmth in our relationships.

Ultimately, gratitude leads us to a more enjoyable life. It reminds us to focus on what matters most and cherish the good things we often overlook. By practicing gratitude consistently, we can overcome negativity, transform our attitude, and bring light and joy into our lives—and the lives of others. Let's choose gratitude and watch the miracles unfold.

7. Self-Pity: Replacing Bitterness With Gratitude

Ungratefulness often traps us in self-pity, where we feel like victims of life's unfairness. In this state, we focus on what we lack, and bitterness begins to take root in our hearts. We feel resentment toward our circumstances, constantly wondering why life feels so hard or why others seem to have it better. This mindset isolates us and pulls us further into negativity, blocking us from seeing the blessings we already have. As the saying beautifully reminds us, "Gratitude turns what we have into enough."

Gratitude offers a way out of the dark spiral of self-pity. By practicing gratitude, we learn to shift our focus from what's missing to what we already have. Instead of dwelling on our struggles, gratitude encourages us to recognize our strengths and the progress we've made, even in difficult situations. As another wise saying goes, *"Gratitude is the antidote to bitterness and resentment."* It dissolves negativity and reminds us of the good that remains in our lives.

When we embrace gratitude, it transforms our perspective and empowers us to move forward. We take control of our feelings, replacing hopelessness with hope and self-worth. Gratitude helps us see ourselves as resilient and capable, able to face challenges with confidence. It reframes our hardships, reminding us that struggles are often opportunities for growth and strength.

Ultimately, gratitude restores joy and gives us a sense of direction. It helps us break free from self-pity and step into a life of purpose and possibility. By focusing on our blessings and accomplishments, we can rise above bitterness and move forward with optimism and courage. Gratitude not only lifts our spirits but also inspires us to live boldly and gratefully in every season of life.

8. Spiritual Disconnection: Renewing Faith Through Gratitude

Ungratefulness creates distance between us and our spiritual beliefs. When we focus on material things, we lose sight of life's deeper meaning and purpose. Gratitude, however, reconnects us with what truly matters. As the quote says, *"Gratitude is the heart's memory."*

By being thankful for life's blessings, we strengthen our spiritual foundation and grow closer to our faith. Gratitude deepens our understanding of purpose and fulfillment, reminding us, *"Gratitude is the fairest blossom which springs from the soul."*

Practicing gratitude helps us find peace and connection in our spiritual journey. It opens our hearts to the divine and brings contentment that material things can never provide. Gratitude brings us back to what life is truly about.

5

GOOD THINGS COME TO GRATEFUL PEOPLE

Gratitude opens the door to good things. When you live with a thankful heart, you attract peace, favor, and joy. Gratitude is not just a feeling—it's a force. It changes your attitude, your atmosphere, and your outcome. The Bible says, *"Give thanks to the Lord, for He is good; His love endures forever"* (**Psalm 107:1**). When you thank God, you invite His goodness into your life. You begin to see blessings you once overlooked. You stop chasing happiness and start choosing it. Grateful people don't wait for perfect conditions—they praise in every season. And that praise brings power. It brings healing, hope, and help. Gratitude is a magnet for miracles. When you are grateful, good things find you.

Grateful people grow, glow, and go forward. They grow in wisdom, glow with joy, and go forward with faith. Gratitude helps you rise above fear, frustration, and failure. It gives you strength to keep going and grace to keep growing. The Bible says, *"In everything give thanks; for this is the will of God in Christ Jesus for you"* (**1 Thessalonians 5:18**). That means thankfulness is not just a suggestion—it's a strategy. It's how you win battles, build peace, and walk in purpose. Grateful people don't just survive—they thrive. They don't just receive—they release blessings to others. Gratitude makes you useful, joyful, and impactful. So if you want good things to come, start with a grateful heart. Because gratitude is the seed—and goodness is the harvest.

Gratitude Attracts Greatness and Great Blessings

Being grateful is one of the most powerful practices you can adopt. It is a life-changing secret that brings joy, love, and peace into your heart. Gratitude helps you see life differently, making even ordinary moments feel extraordinary. It turns what others take for granted into meaningful blessings. The more you practice gratitude, the closer you draw to God—the ultimate Giver of all things. As **Psalm 107:1** reminds us, *"Give thanks to the Lord, for He is good; His love endures forever."*

Gratitude pleases God and touches His heart. Imagine how you feel when someone appreciates the efforts you make for them. It inspires you to do even more for them, doesn't it? The same happens with God. When His children practice gratitude, it brings Him joy and opens the door to even greater blessings. On the other hand, complaining shuts these doors. It blinds us to the good around us and steals the joy God has intended for us. **Philippians 4:6-7** guides us, *"Do not be anxious about anything, but in every situation, by prayer and petition, with thanksgiving, present your requests to God."*

Gratitude transforms each day into an opportunity for joy and peace. Whether it's a Monday, a Sunday, or any other day, remember that every hour is a chance to be grateful. Each day is a miracle and a gift from God. Stop waiting for weekends or special occasions to express joy. As **1 Thessalonians 5:18** instructs, *"Give*

SYAVIHA MULENGYA

thanks in all circumstances; for this is God's will for you in Christ Jesus." Gratitude reminds us that every moment has meaning and every breath is a blessing.

The beauty of gratitude is that it multiplies blessings. It's not about having more but appreciating what you already have. Gratitude opens your eyes to the abundance already in your life. You may not have everything, but what you do have becomes enough. **James 1:17** assures us, *"Every good and perfect gift is from above, coming down from the Father of the heavenly lights."* Count your blessings, and you'll find that they grow.

People who practice gratitude discover hidden joys that others miss. They sleep better, worry less, and approach life with positivity. Gratitude reduces stress and creates an inner peace that surpasses understanding. **Proverbs 17:22** reminds us, *"A cheerful heart is excellent medicine, but a crushed spirit dries up the bones."* Gratitude is a source of healing for the soul and mind.

Stop singing songs of sorrow and start singing songs of success. Know that you are blessed, highly favored, and loved by God. Some people miss their blessings because they do not practice gratitude. Choose gratitude to unlock more beauty and blessings in your life. As **Colossians 3:15** encourages us, *"Let the peace of Christ rule in your hearts, since as members of one body you were called to peace. And be thankful."*

Gratitude Opens Doors

1. Health

Gratitude has a powerful impact on our physical and mental health. When we focus on the good things in our lives, it reduces stress and anxiety, which improves our overall well-being. **Proverbs 17:22** teaches us, *"A cheerful heart is good medicine, but a crushed* spirit dries up the bones." Gratitude encourages us to keep a cheerful heart, which acts as a natural remedy for physical and emotional pain. It strengthens our immune system, helping us fight off illnesses and feel more energized.

Gratitude also inspires us to take care of ourselves. When we appreciate our bodies and the gift of life, we are more motivated to adopt healthy habits. This includes eating nutritious foods, staying active through exercise, and getting enough sleep. These positive habits increase vitality, enabling us to live our best lives. Gratitude transforms self-care from a chore into a joyful act of stewardship over the blessings we've been given.

Finally, gratitude is a shield for our mental health. By maintaining a grateful attitude, we develop a positive outlook that combats feelings of depression and anxiety. **Philippians 4:6-7** reminds us, *"Do not be anxious about anything, but in every situation, by prayer and petition, with thanksgiving, present your requests to God. And the peace of God, which transcends all understanding, will guard your hearts and your minds in Christ Jesus."* Gratitude helps us experience God's peace, protecting both our hearts and minds.

2. Happiness

Gratitude opens the door to happiness by shifting our focus from what we lack to what we have. It helps us find contentment, even in life's simplest moments. **Psalm 107:1** declares, *"Give thanks to the Lord, for He is good; His love endures forever."* When we recognize the goodness of God and His enduring love, our hearts overflow with joy.

Gratitude strengthens relationships by encouraging us to express appreciation for the people in our lives. A kind word or heartfelt "thank you" can deepen our connections and create a sense of belonging. These strong bonds provide us with love and companionship, which are essential for happiness. Sharing gratitude with others brings joy not only to ourselves but to those around us.

Additionally, gratitude helps us savor life's precious moments. By being mindful and present, we can fully enjoy the beauty of each day—a radiant sunrise, a warm hug, or a kind smile. Gratitude teaches us to treasure these experiences, turning ordinary days into joyful memories. Happiness grows when we take the time to be grateful for the blessings we already have.

3. Harmony

Gratitude has the power to bring harmony into our lives and relationships. When we practice thankfulness, it becomes easier to show kindness, compassion, and understanding to the people around us. A heart filled with gratitude shifts our attitude, making us more forgiving and considerate. **Colossians 3:15** reminds us, *"Let the peace of Christ rule in your hearts, since as members of one body you were called to peace. And be thankful."* Gratitude invites this peace into our relationships, fostering unity and strengthening the bonds we share with others.

One of the most beautiful ways gratitude fosters harmony is by resolving conflicts. When we focus on what we appreciate about someone instead of dwelling on frustrations, misunderstandings lose their power. Expressing gratitude allows us to see the good in others and build bridges of peace. A heartfelt "thank you" for someone's efforts or qualities can turn tension into warmth, creating stronger relationships based on mutual respect and care.

Gratitude also promotes teamwork and collaboration. When we take the time to acknowledge and value others' contributions, we create an environment of trust and cooperation. Whether at home, in the workplace, or within the community, this spirit of gratitude unites people and strengthens their ability to work together effectively. It nurtures a culture of encouragement where shared goals are achieved with joy and ease.

Ultimately, gratitude transforms the atmosphere around us. It replaces conflict with connection, tension with togetherness, and isolation with inclusion. By choosing gratitude, we not only bring harmony to our relationships but also create a life filled with peace, happiness, and mutual support. Let gratitude guide your interactions, and watch how it deepens your relationships and fills them with lasting harmony.

4. Hope

Gratitude is a powerful source of hope, as it opens our eyes to the blessings we have already received and the promises of God yet to be fulfilled. When we take a moment to thank God for what He has done in our lives, we are reminded of His faithfulness. **Romans 15:13** tells us, *"May the God of hope fill you with all joy and peace as you trust in Him, so that you may overflow with hope by the power of the Holy Spirit."* Gratitude strengthens our faith and trust in God's plan, allowing us to step into the future with confidence and optimism.

During hard times, gratitude is a tool that helps us persevere. It shifts our focus away from struggles and redirects it toward the positive aspects of life. By appreciating even the smallest blessings, we find the courage to press on. Gratitude reminds us that challenges are not permanent, and better days lie ahead. This sense of resilience grows our inner strength and transforms trials into lessons that prepare us for what's to come.

Moreover, gratitude inspires us to dream boldly and set meaningful goals. When we acknowledge our current blessings, we feel motivated to strive for greater things. Gratitude keeps us grounded while giving us the determination to pursue a life of purpose. Setbacks no longer feel like dead ends; instead, they become stepping stones that guide us toward success. By practicing gratitude, we gain a hopeful perspective that fuels our ambitions.

Gratitude is a gift that connects the past, present, and future. It gives us a deep sense of joy for what we've been given, resilience to face challenges in the present, and hope for the days ahead. As we cultivate a grateful heart, we align ourselves with God's promises, allowing hope to overflow and lead us toward a brighter, more fulfilling future.

5. Humility

Gratitude teaches us humility by helping us realize that every blessing we have is not achieved by our efforts alone but is a gift from God and the kindness of others. When we acknowledge this truth, it softens our hearts and humbles our spirits. **James 4:10** reminds us, *"Humble yourselves before the Lord, and He will lift you up."* Gratitude shows us that we are not self-sufficient and that we deeply rely on God's grace and the support of the people around us.This sense of humility fosters a spirit of service. When we are grateful for the help we've received, we feel inspired to give back and serve others. Gratitude shifts our focus from our own needs to others', fostering selflessness in our hearts. It teaches us to live as Jesus did, caring for others with compassion and kindness.

Additionally, gratitude keeps us grounded. It helps us avoid pride and arrogance by reminding us to appreciate the blessings we often take for granted. When we live with humility, we build genuine relationships based on trust and respect. Humility allows us to live a life of grace and integrity, reflecting God's love in our words and actions.

6. Hospitality

Gratitude opens our hearts to practice hospitality. When we recognize the blessings in our lives, we feel more inclined to share them with others. **Hebrews 13:2** encourages us, *"Do not forget to show hospitality to strangers, for by so doing some people have shown hospitality to angels without knowing it."* A grateful heart welcomes others warmly and creates a space where love and kindness can flourish.

Hospitality strengthens communities by fostering connection and belonging. When we invite others into our homes and our lives, we build a sense of support and togetherness. Gratitude reminds us to value the presence and contributions of others, strengthening the bonds between us.Gratitude also encourages generosity. When we see the abundance in our lives, we are motivated to help those in need, whether through small acts of kindness or larger acts of giving. This generosity not only enriches the lives of others but also brings joy and fulfillment to our own hearts. Practicing hospitality creates a cycle of love and gratitude that makes life richer for everyone involved.

7. Honor

Gratitude teaches us to honor others by showing respect and appreciation for their efforts and presence in our lives. When we express thanks, we acknowledge the value and dignity of those around us. **Romans 12:10** urges us, *"Be devoted to one another in love. Honor one another above yourselves."* Gratitude reflects this devotion by helping us see and celebrate the good in others.

Honor is built on trust and respect, which gratitude helps to cultivate. By appreciating the kindness, support, or guidance others offer, we create a culture of mutual respect. This honor strengthens relationships and fosters a positive and uplifting environment, where everyone feels valued.

Gratitude also enhances our reputation. When people see us as thankful and respectful, they trust us more and admire the attitude we carry. This creates opportunities for personal growth, strengthens bonds with others, and enriches our lives. Honor, rooted in gratitude, transforms how we interact with people and leaves a lasting positive impact on the world around us.

6

GIVING THANKS GLORIFIES GOD

God Loves Gratitude and Expects It

God delights in gratitude. He loves it when we appreciate the blessings He generously gives us, and He expects us to acknowledge His goodness with thankful hearts. The truth is, we don't have to pay for any of the gifts He provides—His grace is entirely free. From the air we breathe to the safety we enjoy, God's blessings are constant and immeasurable. He walks beside us, protects us, works for our benefit, fights battles on our behalf, frees us from danger, and forgives our sins. If we had to pay for even one of these gifts, no one could afford them. Take something as simple as oxygen—if we had to buy it as we do in a hospital, the cost would be staggering. Yet since birth, we have breathed it freely. As **Psalm 107:1** reminds us, *"Give thanks to the Lord, for He is good; His love endures forever."*

God's provision for us goes far beyond what we can ever repay. He is a defender in our struggles, a provider in our need, a guide in uncertain times, and a problem solver for our worries—all without asking for payment. The one thing He asks of us is to honor Him with obedience and gratitude. Recognizing His goodness and worshiping Him is not only an act of faith but also an expression of love that brings glory to His name. **Philippians 4:6-7** reminds us, *"Do not be anxious about anything, but in every situation, by prayer and petition, with thanksgiving, present your requests to God."* Gratitude is how we show our trust in His provision and invite His peace into our lives.

Gratitude is more than a habit—it is a powerful way to deepen our connection with God. When we are thankful, we acknowledge His presence and His works, pleasing Him and drawing closer to His heart. Walking faithfully with Him and waiting patiently for His answers are acts of gratitude that demonstrate our belief in His plans. The more we practice gratitude, the more aware we become of His blessings and the more willing we are to follow His path. **Colossians 3:17** encourages us, *"And whatever you do, whether in word or deed, do it all in the name of the Lord Jesus, giving thanks to God the Father through Him."* Gratitude aligns our actions and our hearts with God's purpose.

Gratitude transforms not just our relationship with God but our entire lives. It changes our perspective, shifting our focus from what we lack to what we already have. This brings joy, peace, and contentment, allowing us to live fully and happily. A thankful heart is a heart that recognizes abundance, no matter the circumstances. Practicing gratitude helps us live according to God's will and experience the fullness of His blessings. As **1 Thessalonians 5:18** teaches us, *"Give thanks in all circumstances; for this is God's will for you in Christ Jesus."* Gratitude is not just a reaction to God's blessings—it is a lifestyle that honors Him and keeps us close to His love. Let gratitude be a daily choice that opens the door to God's grace and goodness.

God Enjoys Our Gratitude

God delights in our gratitude because it acknowledges His goodness, faithfulness, and love. Being thankful to Him is a way to honor His presence in our lives and to recognize that every blessing comes from Him. He freely gives us gifts, such as health, provision, guidance, and forgiveness, all without cost. **Psalm 107:1** declares, *"Give thanks to the Lord, for He is good; His love endures forever."* When we practice gratitude, we show appreciation for His care and provision, strengthening our relationship with Him.

Gratitude also reflects our trust in God's plan. It demonstrates that we believe in His ability to work all things together for our good, even when life is challenging. This confidence pleases God because it shows that we rely on His promises and accept His timing. **Philippians 4:6-7** reassures us, *"Do not be anxious about anything, but in every situation, by prayer and petition, with thanksgiving, present your requests to God."* Gratitude deepens our faith and brings joy to God's heart as He sees His children living in trust and thankfulness.

1. Praise God

Gratitude naturally leads us to praise God for His goodness and greatness. **Psalm 100:4** encourages us, *"Enter His gates with thanksgiving and His courts with praise; give thanks to Him and praise His name."* When we praise God, we acknowledge the marvelous ways He works in our lives and express love and admiration for Him.

Praising God also strengthens our faith. When we recount His deeds and reflect on His blessings, we are reminded of His power and unwavering faithfulness. **Psalm 34:1** declares, *"I will extol the Lord at all times; His praise will always be on my lips."* This act of gratitude and praise deepens our trust in His promises and encourages us to rely on His strength.

Moreover, praising God brings joy to our hearts. It shifts our focus from difficulties to His greatness, filling us with hope, peace, and happiness. **Psalm 95:2** invites us, *"Let us come before Him with thanksgiving and extol Him with music and song."* Through praise, gratitude becomes a celebration of God's love and presence.

2. Please God

Gratitude pleases God because it shows that we recognize and appreciate His blessings. **Hebrews 13:15** reminds us, *"Through Jesus, therefore, let us continually offer to God a sacrifice of praise—the fruit of lips that openly profess His name."* When we openly thank Him, we honor His goodness, and this delights Him.

Gratitude also demonstrates our trust in His plan. By giving thanks in all circumstances, we show our belief in His sovereignty and His ability to work all things for our good. **Romans 8:28** assures us, *"And we know that in all things God works for the good of those who love Him."* Trusting God through gratitude pleases Him deeply, as it reflects our reliance on His wisdom and guidance.

Additionally, gratitude fosters humility, which is pleasing to God. When we acknowledge that our blessings come from Him, we avoid pride and arrogance. Instead, we cultivate a humble heart that aligns with His will. **James 4:10** encourages us, *"Humble yourselves before the Lord, and He will lift you up."* Gratitude keeps us grounded and connected to His grace.

3. Proclaim His Goodness

Gratitude inspires us to proclaim God's goodness to others. When we are thankful, we naturally want to share His blessings and declare His love and faithfulness. **Psalm 105:1** encourages us, *"Give praise to the Lord, proclaim His name; make known among the nations what He has done."* Proclaiming His goodness is a way to testify to His greatness and spread hope.

Sharing gratitude also encourages those around us. When we express thankfulness for God's blessings, we inspire others to reflect on their own and recognize His presence in their lives. This creates a ripple effect of gratitude and praise. **Psalm 96:3** calls us, *"Declare His glory among the nations, His marvelous deeds among all peoples."* By sharing our gratitude, we help others see the beauty of God's works.

Proclaiming His goodness also strengthens our faith. By reflecting on His deeds and expressing thanks, we remind ourselves of His power and trustworthiness. **Psalm 89:1** declares, *"I will sing of the Lord's great love forever; with my mouth I will make your faithfulness known through all generations."* Gratitude reinforces our reliance on His promises and deepens our relationship with Him.

4. Pray

Gratitude strengthens our prayer life by inviting us to thank God for His blessings. When we pray with thanksgiving, we acknowledge His goodness and express our appreciation for all that He has done for us. **Philippians 4:6-7** encourages, *"Do not be anxious about anything, but in every situation, by prayer and petition, with thanksgiving, present your requests to God."* Praying with gratitude brings peace to our hearts, as it reminds us of God's presence and faithfulness in every situation.

SYAVIHA MULENGYA

Gratitude in prayer also shifts our focus from our needs to God's provision. By thanking Him for what we already have, we cultivate contentment and trust in His plan. This trust is pleasing to God and strengthens our faith in Him. **Colossians 4:2** encourages us, *"Devote yourselves to prayer, being watchful and thankful."* Gratitude transforms our prayers into moments of both humility and hope, helping us align our desires with God's will.

Additionally, gratitude in prayer fosters a positive and joyful outlook. It opens our eyes to the many blessings in our lives, encouraging us to approach God with confidence and thankfulness. This attitude of gratitude brings us closer to His heart, filling us with peace and joy. As **1 Thessalonians 5:16-18** advises, *"Rejoice always, pray continually, give thanks in all circumstances; for this is God's will for you in Christ Jesus."*

5. Promote His Name and Presence

Gratitude compels us to share God's blessings with others and proclaim His greatness. When we are thankful, we naturally desire to spread the message of His love and faithfulness to those around us. **Psalm 96:2-3** calls us, *"Sing to the Lord, praise His name; proclaim His salvation day after day. Declare His glory among the nations, His marvelous deeds among all peoples."* Sharing His goodness is a way to testify to His greatness and to promote His presence in the world.

Promoting God's name and presence through gratitude also inspires others. When we share our experiences of thankfulness, we encourage those around us to reflect on their own blessings and recognize God's work in their lives. This creates a ripple effect of thanksgiving and praise, as **Psalm 145:4** declares, *"One generation commends your works to another; they tell of your mighty acts."*

Moreover, proclaiming His name strengthens our own faith. By recounting the blessings we have received and expressing gratitude, we remind ourselves of God's power and goodness. This builds our trust in His promises and strengthens our connection with Him. **Psalm 89:1** affirms, *"I will sing of the Lord's great love forever; with my mouth I will make your faithfulness known through all generations."*

6. Participate in Worship

Gratitude draws us into worship, inspiring us to honor God with our words and hearts. When we acknowledge His blessings, we are moved to praise Him for His goodness and faithfulness. **Psalm 100:2** encourages, *"Worship the Lord with gladness; come before Him with joyful songs."* Participating in worship is an expression of our gratitude and love for God, and it deepens our connection with Him.

Worship also builds our faith as we sing praises and reflect on God's works. As we lift our voices in gratitude, we are reminded of His greatness and the promises He has fulfilled. Psalm 95:6 invites us, *"Come, let us bow down in worship, let us kneel before the Lord our Maker."* Gratitude-filled worship strengthens our trust in His guidance and fills us with hope.

Additionally, worship brings joy and peace to our hearts. It shifts our focus from our worries to God's glory, filling us with hope and comfort. This joy reflects His presence in our lives and our appreciation for His blessings. **Psalm 63:4** beautifully declares, *"I will praise you as long as I live, and in your name I will lift up my hands."*

7. Prophesy Over Our Lives

Gratitude inspires us to speak positive words and declare God's promises over our lives. When we are thankful, we align our words with His will, inviting His blessings into our future. **Proverbs 18:21** reminds us, *"The tongue has the power of life and death, and those who love it will eat its fruit."* Prophesying over our lives reflects our trust in God's plans and His ability to fulfill His promises.

Prophesying also builds faith as we declare His Word and express gratitude for what He will do. **Jeremiah 29:11** assures us, *"For I know the plans I have for you, declares the Lord, plans to prosper you and not to harm you, plans to give you hope and a future."* Gratitude helps us confidently speak blessings and hope over our lives, knowing that God's plan is good.

Moreover, prophesying over our lives brings encouragement and inspiration. It allows us to envision God's blessings and motivates us to pursue His will with confidence. **Romans 15:13** proclaims, *"May the God of hope fill you with all joy and peace as you trust in Him, so that you may overflow with hope by the power of the Holy Spirit."* Gratitude fills our hearts with hope and strengthens our declarations of faith.

8. Profess Success and Victory

Gratitude leads us to declare success and victory in our lives, reminding us of God's promises and His power to bring them to pass. When we give thanks, we proclaim His goodness and speak words of faith that invite His blessings. **1 Corinthians 15:57** encourages, *"But thanks be to God! He gives us the victory through our Lord Jesus Christ."* Professing success and victory aligns our hearts and words with God's will.

Professing success and victory also deepens our faith. Gratitude helps us trust that God is in control and that His plans for us are filled with hope and purpose. **Philippians 4:13** assures us, *"I can do all this through Him who gives me strength."* By declaring

His promises, we show our confidence in His guidance and provision. Professing success and victory fills us with hope and determination. It encourages us to see the possibilities for God's blessings and motivates us to follow His will. **Romans 8:37** declares, *"No, in all these things we are more than conquerors through Him who loved us."* Gratitude inspires us to speak life over our future, trusting in God's promises for success and victory.

7

DON'T OVERLOOK WHAT YOU HAVE

The Cost of Taking Things for Granted

Jackson and Jacky had been married for several years. Jacky, a highly ambitious career woman, was deeply dedicated to her job and often poured most of her time and energy into her work. She found her passion in her profession and prioritized it above everything else, including her marriage. Meanwhile, Jackson valued their relationship. He made an effort to spend time with Jacky and nurture their connection, but he often felt neglected and unappreciated.

The cracks in their marriage widened when Jacky received a promotion. Her new responsibilities at work demanded more of her attention, and she became completely engrossed in her job. In her pursuit of career success, Jacky began to take Jackson for granted. She stopped cooperating in their relationship, emotionally withdrew from him, and even started treating him poorly. She dismissed her responsibilities as a wife and belittled Jackson's

SYAVIHA MULENGYA

contributions, saying, *"You know I earn more than you. If you're not comfortable, you can leave."* Her words cut deeply, leaving Jackson feeling trapped and hurt.

Jackson, committed to saving their marriage, made several attempts to communicate his feelings and improve their relationship. He suggested counseling and tried to express his concerns, but Jacky brushed them aside. Her dismissive attitude left Jackson feeling isolated, unappreciated, and emotionally drained. The emotional abuse he endured took a serious toll on his well-being, and he began to question whether he could continue in such a toxic environment.

Eventually, Jackson reached a breaking point. Realizing that his efforts were not making a difference, he made the hard decision to leave the marriage. He chose to prioritize his mental and emotional health, seeking healing and peace. During this time, Jackson worked on rebuilding his life and gradually recovered from the emotional scars left by the relationship.

As Jackson moved forward, Jacky began to reflect on her actions. She regretted taking Jackson and their love for granted. She realized too late the value of the relationship they once shared. However, by then, Jackson had moved on. He found a new partner, Jessica, who deeply valued and respected him.

Jessica and Jackson built a beautiful and harmonious relationship. They supported each other in every aspect of life, embarking on meaningful projects and growing together personally and professionally. Their mutual appreciation and effort created a firm foundation for love and happiness. They both prioritized their relationship and worked as a team to maintain a fulfilling life.

SYAVIHA MULENGYA

On the other hand, Jacky's life spiraled downward. She lost her job, fell into depression, and developed health problems. Overwhelmed with regret, she tried to interfere in Jackson's new relationship, begging him to return. But Jackson, having endured humiliation and emotional pain, knew he could not go back. He had found peace and happiness in his new life with Jessica.

Jacky's story serves as a powerful reminder of the consequences of taking people and relationships for granted. Loving relationships require effort, respect, and appreciation from both partners. Neglecting these aspects can lead to deep hurt, regret, and broken connections. As **Proverbs 18:22** teaches us, *"He who finds a wife finds what is good and receives favor from the Lord."* Relationships are gifts that should never be taken lightly.

This story reminds us to cherish the people in our lives and to never let ambition or distractions overshadow the love and care we owe to those we hold dear. Gratitude, communication, and mutual respect are essential to maintaining healthy and thriving relationships. Let us strive to value our loved ones each day, so we don't experience the heartache of realizing their worth too late.

What We Forget to Be Thankful For

1. Lament: Regretting What is Lost

When we take things for granted, we often realize their value only after they are gone. This leads to deep regret and sorrow as we reflect on what we could have cherished. **Proverbs 5:11** warns us, *"At the end of your life you will groan, when your flesh and body are spent."* By appreciating our blessings while we have them, we can avoid the heartache of lamenting what we once neglected.

Regret can also weigh heavily on our emotional well-being. Constant feelings of loss and mourning can lead to sadness or even depression. **Psalm 38:6** paints this picture: *"I am bowed down and brought very low; all day long I go about mourning."* Gratitude helps us focus on the positives in our lives and reduces the likelihood of falling into despair.

Furthermore, lamenting the past can prevent us from embracing the future. Dwelling on regrets keeps us stuck, unable to move forward and discover new blessings. **Isaiah 43:18-19** reminds us, *"Forget the former things; do not dwell on the past. See, I am doing a new thing!"* When we live with gratitude, we can look forward with hope instead of being trapped by our regrets.

2. Letting Go of Great Opportunities

When we fail to value what we have, we may let go of great opportunities without even realizing their potential. Taking things for granted makes us blind to the possibilities right in front of us. **Ecclesiastes 9:10** encourages, *"Whatever your hand finds to do, do it with all your might."* Gratitude helps us be mindful and seize the opportunities that God places in our paths.

Missing great opportunities can lead to a life filled with regret. We may look back and wonder how different things could have been if we had acted with appreciation and diligence. **Ephesians 5:15-16** advises, *"Be very careful, then, how you live—not as unwise but as wise, making the most of every opportunity."* Gratitude allows us to stay alert and make the most of what we are given.

Missing chances also impact our future. When we take things for granted, we may not give our best effort or invest in our growth. **Proverbs 10:4** warns, *"Lazy hands make for poverty, but diligent hands bring wealth."* Gratitude motivates us to work hard and value the opportunities we are blessed with.

SYAVIHA MULENGYA

3. Leaving the Best While Chasing More

Taking things for granted often leads us to overlook the blessings in front of us as we search for something "better." This endless pursuit of more leaves us restless and unsatisfied. **Ecclesiastes 4:6** teaches, *"Better one handful with tranquility than two handfuls with toil and chasing after the wind."* By appreciating what we have, we can find peace and contentment.

Leaving behind what is best for the illusion of more often results in disappointment. We may discover that what we were chasing doesn't bring the happiness we hoped for. **Philippians 4:11-12** offers wisdom: *"I have learned to be content whatever the circumstances. I know what it is to be in need, and I know what it is to have plenty."* Gratitude helps us embrace our current blessings and find joy in what is already ours.

Additionally, constantly chasing more can harm our relationships and our health. We may neglect the people and things that truly matter in life. **Proverbs 15:16** reminds us, *"Better a little with the fear of the Lord than great wealth with turmoil."* Gratitude keeps us grounded, helping us cherish what truly matters.

4. Lacking Fulfillment in Life

Taking things for granted robs us of the ability to feel truly fulfilled. When we fail to appreciate our blessings, we are left feeling empty and dissatisfied. **Ecclesiastes 6:9** puts it plainly: *"Better what the eye sees than the roving of the appetite. This too is meaningless, a chasing after the wind."* Gratitude helps us find satisfaction in the present moment and the blessings God has already provided.

A lack of fulfillment affects our mental and emotional health. Feelings of emptiness and discontent can lead to anxiety and depression. But **Psalm 107:9** promises us this: *"For He satisfies the thirsty and fills the hungry with good things."* By practicing gratitude, we fill our hearts with peace and joy, appreciating what God has already given us.

Finally, a lack of fulfillment can undermine our motivation and sense of purpose. When we are constantly dissatisfied, it becomes harder to achieve our goals or enjoy the journey of life. **Proverbs 13:4** reminds us, *"A sluggard's appetite is never filled, but the desires of the diligent are fully satisfied."* Gratitude fuels our diligence, helping us stay motivated and fulfilled as we walk in God's purpose for our lives.

Taking things for granted leads to lament, missed opportunities, dissatisfaction, and emptiness. But practicing gratitude transforms how we view our blessings, relationships, and circumstances. By appreciating what God has given us, we avoid regret and find peace, contentment, and joy in every season of life. Let us choose to value the present and trust in God's provision for a brighter, more fulfilling future.

5. Live an Unhappy Life

Failing to appreciate our blessings can leave us feeling constantly dissatisfied and unhappy. When we take things for granted, we lose sight of the joy and goodness in our lives and focus instead on what we lack. **Proverbs 15:15** warns, *"All the days of the oppressed are wretched, but the cheerful heart has a continual feast."* Gratitude is the key to cultivating a cheerful heart and finding joy in everyday life.

Living an unhappy life can strain our relationships and affect our mental and emotional health. When we are unhappy, it's harder to connect with others and enjoy meaningful interactions.

Ecclesiastes 3:12-13 reminds us, *"I know that there is nothing better for people than to be happy and to do good while they live. That each of them may eat and drink, and find satisfaction in all their toil—this is the gift of God."* Practicing gratitude helps us see happiness as a gift from God and improves our relationships and overall well-being.

An unhappy life can also hinder our ability to pursue our goals and dreams. When dissatisfaction takes over, it drains us of the motivation and energy needed to move forward. **Psalm 37:4** encourages us, *"Take delight in the Lord, and He will give you the desires of your heart."* Gratitude helps us focus on God's blessings and find the joy and determination to achieve our aspirations.

6. Look Down on Blessings and Others

Taking things for granted can cause us to undervalue our blessings and the people around us. Instead of seeing their worth, we may treat them with disrespect or indifference. **James 2:1** advises, *"My brothers and sisters, believers in our glorious Lord Jesus Christ must not show favoritism."* Gratitude helps us appreciate and respect the blessings and people in our lives.

Looking down on what we have can lead to entitlement and arrogance. We may start to believe we deserve more, ignoring the value of what God has already provided. Proverbs 16:18 warns, *"Pride goes before destruction, a haughty spirit before a fall."* Gratitude keeps us humble and helps us recognize the worth of our blessings. Treating others with disrespect can also damage our relationships and create unnecessary conflict. **Romans 12:10** encourages, *"Be devoted to one another in love. Honor one another above yourselves."* By valuing and honoring others, we build stronger connections and foster harmony in our relationships.

SYAVIHA MULENGYA

7. Land into Problems and Trouble

Taking things for granted can lead to poor decision-making and unnecessary trouble. When we fail to appreciate our blessings, we may act recklessly and face negative consequences. **Proverbs 19:3** warns, *"A person's own folly leads to their ruin, yet their heart rages against the Lord."* Gratitude helps us make wise choices and avoid trouble by keeping our hearts focused on God's provision.

Trouble can take a toll on our mental and emotional well-being, leaving us stressed and regretful. **Psalm 34:17** provides hope: *"The righteous cry out, and the Lord hears them; He delivers them from all their troubles."* By practicing gratitude, we stay connected to God's guidance, reducing the likelihood of falling into unnecessary challenges.

Problems can also interfere with our ability to achieve our goals. Constant setbacks and difficulties can drain our motivation and leave us feeling lost. **Proverbs 3:5-6** encourages, *"Trust in the Lord with all your heart and lean not on your own understanding; in all your ways submit to Him, and He will make your paths straight."* Gratitude helps us trust in God's plan and navigate life's challenges with faith and wisdom.

8. Languish in Dissatisfaction

Taking things for granted can leave us languishing in dissatisfaction and discontent. Instead of appreciating our blessings, we may feel constantly unfulfilled and disconnected from joy. **Ecclesiastes 2:11** laments, *"Yet when I surveyed all that my hands had done and what I had toiled to achieve, everything was meaningless, a chasing after the wind; nothing was gained under the sun."* Gratitude helps us find meaning and fulfillment by focusing on God's gifts rather than what we lack.

SYAVIHA MULENGYA

Languishing can harm our mental and emotional health. Feelings of emptiness and hopelessness may arise, leading to depression or anxiety. **Psalm 42:11** encourages us to put our hope in God: *"Why, my soul, are you downcast? Why so disturbed within me? Put your hope in God, for I will yet praise Him, my Savior and my God."* Gratitude helps us reconnect with God's peace and find comfort in His promises.

Discontentment can also prevent us from pursuing our goals and living a fulfilling life. When we are constantly dissatisfied, we may lose the motivation to move forward. **Proverbs 13:12** reminds us, *"Hope deferred makes the heart sick, but a longing fulfilled is a tree of life."* Gratitude keeps us focused on our aspirations and fuels our hope, leading to a life of purpose and fulfillment.

Taking things for granted creates unhappiness, damages relationships, and leads to missed opportunities and challenges. But gratitude offers an antidote, helping us value our blessings, trust God's plan, and find joy and peace in every circumstance. Let us choose gratitude and experience the abundant life God has prepared for us.

8

FOCUS ON BLESSINGS, NOT BURDENS

1. Think of Your Blessings and Recognize Them

Before you complain, stop and count your blessings. Take a moment to reflect on all the good things in your life, even the little things you may take for granted. **James 1:17** reminds us, *"Every good and perfect gift is from above, coming down from the Father of the heavenly lights."* By recognizing these blessings, you shift your focus from what's missing to what you already have.

Acknowledging your blessings helps you develop a thankful heart. It allows you to see the abundance in your life and appreciate everything God has provided. **Psalm 103:2** encourages us, *"Praise the Lord, my soul, and forget not all His benefits."* Gratitude not only brings joy but also helps you feel content with what you have.

Reflecting on your blessings can also change how you view challenges. It helps you realize that even in hard times, there's still good to be found. **Philippians 4:8** advises us to think about *"whatever is true, whatever is noble, whatever is right, whatever is pure, whatever is lovely, whatever is admirable… if anything is excellent or praiseworthy."* Focusing on the positives brings peace and hope to your heart.

2. Thank God and Thank People

Gratitude starts with recognizing God as the giver of all blessings. Take time to thank Him for His constant care and provision. **Psalm 136:1** reminds us, *"Give thanks to the Lord, for He is good. His love endures forever."* By thanking God, you strengthen your relationship with Him and show appreciation for His goodness.

Equally important is expressing gratitude to the people in your life. A simple "thank you" can go a long way in strengthening relationships and fostering kindness. **Colossians 3:15** encourages us, *"Let the peace of Christ rule in your hearts, since as members of one body you were called to peace. And be thankful."* Gratitude builds trust and helps create a supportive environment.

Your thankfulness can also inspire others. When you thank God and people, you set an example of kindness and appreciation. **1 Thessalonians 5:18** advises us, *"Give thanks in all circumstances; for this is God's will for you in Christ Jesus."* Practicing gratitude spreads positivity and encourages others to embrace it too.

3. Talk to Yourself

Before you complain, take a moment to talk to yourself. Ask yourself if complaining will truly help the situation or if there's a better way to respond. **Proverbs 4:23** reminds us, *"Above all else, guard your heart, for everything you do flows from it."* Protecting your heart and mind from negativity allows you to approach challenges more constructively.

Talking to yourself can also lead to solutions. Instead of focusing on what's wrong, think about what actions you can take to improve the situation. **Philippians 4:13** encourages us, *"I can do all this through Him who gives me strength."* With God's help, you can face challenges with courage and positivity. Self-reflection leads to growth. By examining your emotions and responses, you can learn better ways to handle difficulties. **Psalm 139:23-24** says, *"Search me, God, and know my heart; test me and know my anxious thoughts. See if there is any offensive way in me, and lead me in the way everlasting."* Seeking God's guidance helps you respond with wisdom and grace.

4. Treasure What You Have

Appreciate the blessings God has placed in your life. Treasure your relationships, possessions, and experiences as gifts from Him. **Matthew 6:21** reminds us, *"For where your treasure is, there your heart will be also."* By treasuring what you have, you cultivate a heart filled with gratitude and contentment.

Valuing your blessings brings joy and satisfaction. It helps you find happiness in simple moments and see beauty in everyday life. **Ecclesiastes 3:13** tells us, *"That each of them may eat and drink, and find satisfaction in all their toil—this is the gift of God."* Gratitude transforms ordinary moments into sources of happiness.

Treasure your relationships as well. Expressing appreciation for the people in your life strengthens bonds and deepens connections. **Romans 12:10** advises, *"Be devoted to one another in love. Honor one another above yourselves."* By valuing your loved ones, you create a community of support and love.

5. Try to Look Around and See the Good

Before you complain, take a moment to observe the blessings all around you. Notice the beauty of nature, the kindness of others, and the opportunities in your life. **Psalm 19:1** proclaims, *"The heavens declare the glory of God; the skies proclaim the work of His hands."* By looking around, you'll find countless reasons to be grateful.

Gaining perspective helps you see beyond your current struggles. **Romans 1:20** reminds us, *"For since the creation of the world God's invisible qualities—His eternal power and divine nature—have been clearly seen, being understood from what has been made."* Observing God's creation inspires hope and reminds you of His power and care. Looking around helps you appreciate the blessings you may have overlooked. It reminds you to be mindful and present in the moment. **Psalm 118:24** joyfully declares, *"This is the day the Lord has made; let us rejoice and be glad in it."* By noticing the surrounding good, you nurture a heart of gratitude and joy.

6. Train Your Mind to See the Miracles

Learning to see the miracles in your life is a transformative practice. It encourages you to focus on the positives and notice the extraordinary in the ordinary. **Romans 12:2** urges us, *"Do not conform to the pattern of this world, but be transformed by the renewing of your mind."* By renewing your mind, you can cultivate gratitude and see God's hand in every aspect of your life.

When you train your mind to appreciate miracles, you open your heart to joy and wonder. Even small blessings, like a sunrise or the kindness of a friend, become a source of happiness. **Psalm 77:14** acknowledges, *"You are the God who performs miracles; You* *display Your power among the peoples."* Recognizing these everyday wonders strengthens your faith and trust in God's goodness.

Seeing miracles also improves your overall well-being. It reduces stress, lifts your spirits, and promotes a positive mindset. **Philippians 4:8** encourages us to think about, *"whatever is true, whatever is noble, whatever is right, whatever is pure, whatever is lovely, whatever is admirable—if anything is excellent or praiseworthy."* By focusing on these qualities, you can experience peace, contentment, and a renewed sense of joy.

7. Testify the Goodness

Sharing the goodness of God is a powerful way to spread gratitude and inspire others. By testifying about the blessings in your life, you encourage those around you to see their own gifts and deepen their faith. **Psalm 107:2** says, *"Let the redeemed of the Lord tell their story—those He redeemed from the hand of the foe."* When you share God's works, you reflect His glory and bring hope to others.

Testifying creates a ripple effect of gratitude and positivity. When you express thankfulness, you encourage others to adopt the same attitude. **Hebrews 10:24-25** calls us to *"spur one another on toward love and good deeds, not giving up meeting together... but encouraging one another."* By sharing your experiences, you help foster a supportive and grateful community built on faith and mutual appreciation.

Additionally, sharing God's goodness strengthens your own faith. Reflecting on His blessings reminds you of His faithfulness and deepens your trust in His promises. **Psalm 9:1** beautifully declares, *"I will give thanks to you, Lord, with all my heart; I will tell of all your* *wonderful deeds."* As you testify, you honor God and inspire others to see His love and care in their own lives.

9

THE BEST WAY TO START YOUR DAY

Starting your day with gratitude is a wonderful way to begin your morning and set the tone for the day. Waking up is a miracle in itself, and ending a day safely is a blessing. Recognize that it takes God's hand to sustain you and bring you to a new day. What God desires from you is a simple "thank you." **Psalm 118:24** reminds us, *"This is the day the Lord has made; let us rejoice and be glad in it."* Acknowledging the gift of a new day honors God and allows you to fully appreciate the blessings He has provided.

Gratitude opens your heart to see life's many blessings, both big and small. When you start your day with thankfulness, it's as if you are unlocking a treasure chest filled with joy, peace, and hope. **Philippians 4:6-7** encourages, *"Do not be anxious about anything, but in every situation, by prayer and petition, with thanksgiving, present your requests to God. And the peace of God, which transcends all understanding, will guard your hearts and your* *minds in Christ Jesus."* Beginning your day with gratitude invites God's presence and peace to guide you.

Gratitude also creates a heart that stays connected to God throughout the day. When you are thankful, you acknowledge His blessings and invite Him to work even more in your life. **Colossians 3:15** advises, *"Let the peace of Christ rule in your hearts, since as members of one body you were called to peace. And be thankful."* This attitude helps you notice God's hand in everything you encounter during the day.

Never let complaints or a negative attitude take over. Many people plan for tomorrow but do not live to see it. Waking up is a blessing you should never take for granted. Treasure it, enjoy it, and thank God for it. **Proverbs 3:5-6** reminds us, *"Trust in the Lord with all your heart and lean not on your own understanding; in all your ways submit to Him, and He will make your paths straight."* By starting your day with gratitude, you not only honor God but also welcome His guidance, favor, and protection into your life.

Start Your Day with Gratitude

1. Boost Your Mood. Gratitude has the power to boost your mood and start your day on a positive note. When you focus on your blessings, you cultivate a heart filled with joy and peace. **Psalm 118:24** says, *"This is the day the Lord has made; let us rejoice and be glad in it."* Recognizing God's goodness brightens your day and lifts your spirit.

Gratitude also helps reduce stress and anxiety, giving you a sense of calm to face the day. **Philippians 4:6-7** reminds us, *"Do not be anxious about anything, but in every situation, by prayer and petition, with thanksgiving, present your requests to God."* A heart filled with gratitude is a heart ready to embrace the day.

2. Brighten Your Day. When you begin your day with gratitude, it's easier to notice and appreciate the good things around you. Gratitude shifts your perspective, helping you see beauty and joy in life's simplest moments. **Psalm 92:1-2** declares, *"It is good to praise the Lord and make music to your name, O Most High, proclaiming your love in the morning and your faithfulness at night."*

Appreciating your blessings creates positivity, making even ordinary days brighter. **Colossians 3:15** encourages, *"Let the peace of Christ rule in your hearts... And be thankful."* Gratitude illuminates your path and fills your heart with peace.

3. Build Your Spirit. Gratitude builds your spirit by reminding you of God's presence and faithfulness. Starting your day with a thankful heart strengthens your trust in His plan. **Psalm 103:2** says, *"Praise the Lord, my soul, and forget not all His benefits."* Gratitude connects you to God and fills you with His love and hope.

When your spirit is uplifted, you can face challenges with renewed strength. **Romans 15:13** offers encouragement: *"May the God of hope fill you with all joy and peace as you trust in Him."* Gratitude transforms your outlook and strengthens your relationship with God.

4. Build Strong Relationships. Expressing gratitude strengthens relationships by fostering appreciation and kindness. Saying "thank you" to the people around you creates deeper bonds and a sense of connection. **1 Thessalonians 5:18** reminds us, *"Give thanks in all circumstances; for this is God's will for you in Christ Jesus."*

Thankfulness fosters trust, understanding, and respect —the foundation of healthy relationships. **Romans 12:10** teaches us, *"Be devoted to one another in love. Honor one another above* *yourselves."* Gratitude builds meaningful relationships and a sense of community.

5. Bring More Blessings to You. When you are grateful for what you have, you invite even more blessings into your life. A thankful heart is open to receiving God's abundance. **James 1:17** reminds us, *"Every good and perfect gift is from above, coming down from the Father of the heavenly lights."* Gratitude attracts positivity and abundance. **Psalm 107:1** encourages, *"Give thanks to the Lord, for He is good; His love endures forever."* By focusing on what you have, you welcome God's generosity and goodness into your life.

6. Banish Bad and Negative Thoughts. Gratitude helps eliminate negative emotions by redirecting your focus to the good in your life. Starting your day with thankfulness reduces the impact of worry and stress. **Philippians 4:8** encourages, *"Finally, brothers and sisters, whatever is true, whatever is noble, whatever is right, whatever is pure, whatever is lovely, whatever is admirable—if anything is excellent or praiseworthy—think about such things."* A grateful heart is a peaceful heart. It allows you to approach life's challenges with confidence and positivity. **Psalm 34:1** declares, *"I will extol the Lord at all times; His praise will always be on my lips."*

7. Beautify Your Life and the Lives of Others. Gratitude brings beauty to your life and to the lives of those around you. When you express thankfulness, you create an uplifting atmosphere. **Proverbs 15:13** reminds us, *"A happy heart makes the face cheerful, but heartache crushes the spirit."* Sharing gratitude inspires others to appreciate their blessings, creating a ripple effect of positivity. **Hebrews 10:24-25** advises, *"Let us consider how we may spur one another on toward love and good deeds."* Gratitude makes life more beautiful for everyone.

SYAVIHA MULENGYA

8. Boom Your Life Starting your day with gratitude can transform your life, filling it with joy and purpose. Gratitude enhances your mental and physical health, increases resilience, and helps you achieve your goals. **Psalm 37:4** promises, *"Take delight in the Lord, and He will give you the desires of your heart."*

A thankful heart leads to a fulfilling and prosperous life. **Proverbs 3:5-6** encourages us, *"Trust in the Lord with all your heart and lean not on your own understanding; in all your ways submit to Him, and He will make your paths straight."* Gratitude paves the way for a life overflowing with blessings and success.

Starting your day with gratitude is the key to experiencing God's peace, joy, and favor. It sets a positive tone, strengthens your faith, and enriches your relationships and well-being. Let gratitude become the foundation of your mornings, and watch how it transforms every aspect of your life.

10

LET THEM KNOW YOU'RE GRATEFUL

Thanking people is a wonderful act that shows kindness and builds strong relationships. The Bible encourages us to be thankful. In Colossians 3:15, it says, *"And be thankful."* When we express gratitude, we follow God's word, which helps us live peacefully with others. Treating people kindly, speaking to them nicely, and recognizing their efforts make them feel appreciated. Everyone wants to feel loved and noticed. Simple acts of gratitude can make a big difference. They not only make others happy but also bring joy to our own hearts.

Good work takes a lot of effort, commitment, and time. It is important to notice and appreciate such hard work. When we thank people, it shows them that their efforts are valuable and meaningful. The Bible reminds us to encourage and build each other up in 1 Thessalonians 5:11. Saying "thank you" inspires people to keep doing good things because they feel recognized. It creates a positive connection between people and builds trust.

Gratitude helps us work better together and shows the love of God to those around us.

In life, it is important to treat others the way we want to be treated. Jesus taught us this in Matthew 7:12 when He said, "Do to others what you would have them do to you." If we want to feel loved and appreciated, we should start by loving and appreciating others. Gratitude opens hearts and creates opportunities for more kindness. When we thank others, we reflect God's love through our actions, helping to deepen relationships and spread happiness. It reminds everyone of their worth and value in this world.

When people are not appreciated, they may feel unimportant, discouraged, or even sad. Relationships can suffer without gratitude because people feel that their efforts do not matter. Thanking someone helps them feel seen and valued. It also supports their emotional and mental well-being. In Proverbs 12:25, the Bible says, *"Anxiety weighs down the heart, but a kind word cheers it up."* Gratitude can lift a heavy heart and bring hope, encouragement, and motivation to others. It strengthens bonds and reminds us all of the power of kindness.

We live in a world where people often focus on mistakes and negativity, forgetting the many good things others do. Gratitude reminds us to celebrate the good in others. Thanking someone shows that you are kind, caring, and thoughtful. It builds peace and harmony, inspiring people to do even more. Gratitude enriches relationships, creates lasting connections, and empowers individuals. When we thank people, we bring love into the world and follow God's teaching to appreciate His blessings. Let us always remember to thank and cherish those around us.

SYAVIHA MULENGYA

Kindness Deserves Thanks

Thanking people is a simple act with powerful effects. The words "thank you" might be small, but they mean a lot, do a lot, and can change lives. They show love, support, and recognition, which we all need to feel valued. Both children and adults enjoy hearing those words, as they bring smiles, uplift hearts, and show appreciation. Saying "thank you" also helps build a positive and supportive environment wherever we are. As Colossians 3:17 says, *"Whatever you do, whether in word or deed, do it all in the name of the Lord Jesus, giving thanks to God the Father through him."*

When we thank others, we reflect kindness and brighten their day. These simple words strengthen relationships and bring people closer together. A sincere "thank you" not only makes others feel appreciated but also helps us focus on the good things in life. It is a way to live out God's teachings by spreading love, building harmony, and strengthening bonds. Let us now look at the benefits of thanking people.

The Power of Saying Thanks

1. Connect

Thanking people helps to build and strengthen connections between individuals. It shows others that we value and appreciate them, creating deeper relationships. Gratitude opens the door to better communication and trust. In Proverbs 17:17, it says, *"A friend loves at all times."* By thanking others, we nurture friendships and make them stronger. In our families, workplaces, and communities, expressing gratitude brings people together and builds harmony.

When we thank people, it develops unity and helps to establish mutual respect. Everyone wants to feel recognized and included,

SYAVIHA MULENGYA

and a simple "thank you" can make a big difference. It bridges the gap between strangers, colleagues, or even loved ones. Through gratitude, we reflect God's love, strengthening our bonds with those around us. It reminds us that we are all part of a larger community where kindness and appreciation thrive.

Thanking others also deepens our relationship with God, as it aligns with His teachings. When we thank the people around us, we show Him that we value the blessings He has placed in our lives. Gratitude honors Him and brings His love into our relationships. This act of connection can transform ordinary moments into meaningful ones.

2. Care

Saying "thank you" is a way to show care and compassion for others. It tells them that their efforts matter and that they are appreciated. Care is at the heart of God's teachings. In 1 Peter 5:7, it says, *"Cast all your anxiety on him because he cares for you."* Just as God cares for us, we are called to care for others, and expressing gratitude is one way to do so.

When we thank someone, we acknowledge their hard work and sacrifices. This not only uplifts their spirits but also inspires them to continue their efforts. Gratitude reminds them that their contributions make a difference. It creates an atmosphere of encouragement where people feel supported and valued.

Caring for others through gratitude strengthens relationships and fosters love. It allows us to share God's kindness with the people in our lives. Saying "thank you" is a small yet meaningful way to bring His light into their hearts. It builds a foundation of love and respect, helping to create a world where kindness and compassion shine.

3. Celebrate

Thanking people is a way to celebrate their achievements and efforts. It shows that we notice and appreciate the good things they do. In Philippians 4:4, it says, *"Rejoice in the Lord always. I will say it again: Rejoice!"* Gratitude is an act of joy and celebration that uplifts both the giver and the receiver.

When we take the time to say "thank you," we highlight the positive actions of others. This encourages them to keep striving and doing their best. Celebrating their efforts motivates them and reminds them of their worth. It also creates moments of joy and togetherness, bringing people closer.

Gratitude celebrates not only what others have done but also the blessings in our lives. It helps us focus on the good, even in difficult times. By thanking people, we share in their happiness and spread positivity. This act of celebration aligns with God's call to rejoice and give thanks in all circumstances.

4. Comfort

A simple "thank you" can bring comfort to someone who may feel unappreciated or unnoticed. It reassures them that their efforts are seen and valued. The Bible reminds us in 2 Corinthians 1:4 that God comforts us so we can comfort others: *"He comforts us in all our troubles so that we can comfort those in any trouble."* Gratitude is one way to extend this comfort to others.

When we thank people, we provide them with emotional support and encouragement. It can lift their spirits and remind them of their importance. Gratitude has the power to brighten someone's day and ease their worries. A kind word can make a world of difference for someone who feels down or unappreciated.

Comforting others through gratitude strengthens relationships and fosters trust. It creates a safe space where people feel valued and understood. By thanking them, we offer them a sense of peace and belonging, reflecting God's love in our actions.

5. Cheer Up Someone

Gratitude is a wonderful way to bring joy and cheer into someone's life. A heartfelt "thank you" can brighten their day and make them feel good about themselves. In Proverbs 12:25, it says, *"Anxiety weighs down the heart, but a kind word cheers it up."* A simple act of gratitude can lift someone's spirits and bring hope to their heart.

When we thank people, we remind them of the positive impact they have on our lives. This act of kindness encourages them and helps them see their worth. Gratitude creates a ripple effect of positivity, spreading joy to those around us. It's a small gesture that can have a big impact on someone's emotional well-being.

Cheering up others through gratitude reflects God's teachings of love and compassion. It shows them that they are cared for and valued. By brightening their day, we share God's light and create moments of happiness and connection.

6. Compliment

Thanking someone is a form of complimenting their efforts and achievements. It shows that we recognize and admire their contributions. The Bible encourages us to build each other up in Ephesians 4:29, which says, *"Do not let any unwholesome talk come out of your mouths, but only what is helpful for building others up."* Gratitude is a way to lift others through kind words.

SYAVIHA MULENGYA

When we thank people, we highlight their strengths and talents. This boosts their confidence and encourages them to keep doing their best. Compliments through gratitude inspire people and remind them of their abilities. It creates an atmosphere of positivity and motivation.

Gratitude as a compliment strengthens relationships and fosters mutual respect. It shows that we value the unique contributions of others and are thankful for their presence in our lives. This act of appreciation brings us closer and reflects God's love and grace.

7. Cultivate

Gratitude helps to cultivate a spirit of kindness, love, and appreciation. It fosters positive relationships and encourages growth. In Galatians 6:9, the Bible says, *"Let us not become weary in doing good, for at the proper time we will reap a harvest if we do not give up."* Thanking others helps to nurture their efforts and inspires them to continue doing good.

When we express gratitude, we create an environment where kindness and appreciation thrive. It motivates others to contribute and builds a culture of positivity. Gratitude cultivates a sense of belonging and connection, enriching our relationships and communities.

Cultivating gratitude helps us grow in our faith and align with God's teachings. It reminds us to appreciate the blessings in our lives and to share His love with those around us. Through gratitude, we plant seeds of kindness that can bloom into lasting harmony and joy.

Let us always remember that thanking people is more than just a polite gesture; it is a reflection of God's love. It connects us, shows

SYAVIHA MULENGYA

care, celebrates achievements, brings comfort, cheers others, compliments efforts, and cultivates a spirit of gratitude. In all that we do, may we follow the word of God and give thanks with joyful hearts.

11

SAY THANK YOU TO
YOURSELF

Thanking yourself is very important because it helps you to see your value and take care of your emotional well-being. Most of the time, we expect love and appreciation from others, but we forget to give it to ourselves. Learning to thank yourself is part of learning self-love. It means accepting who you are, admiring the way you look, and appreciating your efforts and abilities. You may not be perfect, but you are priceless. As Psalm 139:14 says, *"I praise you because I am fearfully and wonderfully made."* Be grateful for the person God has created you to be, and focus on living a peaceful and joyful life that starts with loving yourself.

Thanking yourself also means recognizing the good you are doing, even with your weaknesses. Everyone has flaws, but that doesn't mean you should be harsh on yourself. Some people struggle to accept themselves and may focus only on their failures. Instead, thank yourself for trying your best and for the steps you take every day to improve. In 2 Corinthians 12:9, it says, *"My grace*
SYAVIHA MULENGYA

is sufficient for you, for my power is made perfect in weakness." God reminds us that we can find strength and hope even in our imperfections.

Giving yourself thanks is one of the greatest gifts you can give. Often, we spend time, energy, and money on others but forget to appreciate our own efforts. It's important to take a moment to praise yourself and recognize your hard work. This is not selfish—it is necessary for growth and self-confidence. When you thank yourself, you are showing that you value who you are. As Proverbs 19:8 says, *"The one who gets wisdom loves life; the one who cherishes understanding will soon prosper."* Appreciating yourself is part of building a better life.

Thanking yourself is also a way to motivate and inspire yourself. When you appreciate what you do, you feel encouraged to keep going and to aim for even greater things. Gratitude helps you celebrate your progress and focus on your goals. It's a reminder that your efforts matter and that you have the ability to achieve more. As Philippians 4:13 says, *"I can do all this through him who gives me strength."* Thanking yourself helps you to see the amazing potential God has placed in you and inspires you to live a full and joyful life.

Celebrate Yourself

1. Speak Kind Words to Yourself

Speaking kind words to yourself is one of the simplest yet most powerful ways to nurture self-love and build inner strength. Instead of criticizing yourself for mistakes, focus on your accomplishments and positive traits. Remind yourself that you are valuable, capable, and worthy of love. Words have the power to shape your emotions and perspective, so choose words that bring healing and encouragement. As the Bible says in Proverbs 16:24, *"Gracious words are a honeycomb, sweet to the soul and healing to the bones."* Start your day by speaking kindly to yourself and affirming your worth.

When you choose to speak kind words, you reinforce positivity in your life. This practice not only boosts your confidence but also helps you stay motivated even during difficult times. Remember that no one is perfect, and God's grace is sufficient for you. When you speak kindness over your life, you align your thoughts with God's love and truth. Treat yourself with the same compassion you would offer a friend, and you will see the difference it makes in your self-esteem and mindset.

2. See Your Progress

Taking the time to reflect on your progress is essential for personal growth and self-appreciation. Life is a journey, and every step you take, no matter how small, matters. Instead of dwelling on what you haven't achieved, focus on what you have accomplished. Look back and see how far you've come, and let that motivate you to keep moving forward. In Galatians 6:4, the Bible says, *"Each one should test their own actions. Then they can take pride in themselves."* Recognizing your progress helps you stay encouraged and thankful for your journey.

Seeing your progress also reminds you to celebrate the good in your life. It's easy to get caught up in the daily grind and overlook the victories you've achieved. By acknowledging your efforts and growth, you build a habit of gratitude and positivity. This not only uplifts your spirit but also keeps you focused on your goals. Take pride in your hard work, and trust that every step you take brings you closer to the person God created you to be.

3. Spoil Yourself

Taking time to spoil yourself is a wonderful way to show self-love and appreciation. It doesn't mean being extravagant; it means doing something special to reward yourself for your hard work and dedication. Treat yourself to a favorite meal, a relaxing day off, or even a small gift that brings you joy. In Ecclesiastes 3:13, it says, *"Find satisfaction in all their toil—this is the gift of God."* Spoiling yourself reminds you to enjoy life's blessings and take care of your well-being.

Spoiling yourself also helps recharge your energy and keep you motivated. Life can be demanding, and it's easy to get burned out when you're constantly giving to others or working hard. Rewarding yourself creates balance and helps you remember your own happiness. It's a reminder that your efforts are valued, and you deserve to enjoy the fruits of your labor. Take time to spoil yourself, and let it renew your strength and joy.

4. Say Thank You Again and Again

Thanking yourself regularly is a powerful habit that strengthens your self-esteem and gratitude. Every time you achieve something, whether it's big or small, take a moment to say "thank you" to yourself. This simple act reinforces the effort you put into your life and inspires you to keep going. In 1 Thessalonians 5:18, it says, *"Give thanks in all circumstances."* Practicing gratitude toward yourself helps you recognize the value of your actions and builds a positive mindset.

Saying "thank you" to yourself again and again also creates a sense of appreciation for your journey. It reminds you to focus on what you've accomplished rather than what you lack. Gratitude has the power to uplift your spirit and keep you motivated. Make it a daily habit to thank yourself for your efforts, and you'll find that it encourages you to aim higher and dream bigger.

5. Smile

Smiling is a simple yet effective way to brighten your day and remind yourself of life's joys. When you smile, you release positivity and hope into your life, even during challenging moments. A smile is a gesture of self-love that reflects your inner strength and happiness. In Proverbs 15:13, the Bible says, *"A happy heart makes the face cheerful."* Smiling is a way to show yourself that you are proud of who you are and the progress you've made.

A smile also has the power to change your perspective. Even if you don't feel like smiling at first, the act itself can lift your mood and remind you to focus on the good. Smiling at yourself in the mirror or after accomplishing something encourages self-love and gratitude. It's a small yet meaningful way to celebrate yourself and the blessings God has given you.

6. Show Appreciation

Appreciating yourself is about recognizing your worth and the effort you put into your life. Take a moment to acknowledge the hard work, sacrifices, and dedication that have brought you to where you are today. Gratitude toward yourself builds confidence and reminds you of your strength. In Psalm 107:1, it says, *"Give thanks to the Lord, for he is good; his love endures forever."* Just as we thank God for His goodness, we should also appreciate ourselves as part of His creation.

Showing appreciation to yourself also helps you focus on the positives rather than the negatives. It's easy to be critical of yourself, but gratitude shifts your perspective and builds self-compassion.

When you show yourself appreciation, you create an atmosphere of encouragement and love. It's a way of acknowledging that you are doing your best and that your efforts are meaningful.

7. Salute Yourself

Saluting yourself means honoring the person you are becoming and recognizing your journey with pride. It's not about being arrogant—it's about celebrating your growth and resilience. Stand tall and acknowledge the challenges you've faced and overcome. In Jeremiah 29:11, it says, *"I have plans to prosper you and not to harm you, plans to give you hope and a future."* Saluting yourself is a way to embrace the plans God has for you and to trust in His purpose.

When you salute yourself, you inspire confidence and strength. It's a way of reminding yourself that you are capable and worthy of achieving great things. This act of self-recognition motivates you to keep moving forward and believe in your potential. Salute yourself with gratitude and pride, and you'll see how much you've grown in faith and determination.

12

YOU HAVE THE BEST

Cherishing your blessings means holding them close to your heart and recognizing their true value. It is about appreciating the good things in your life and understanding how they positively impact you. When you cherish your blessings, it helps you stay focused on the good rather than the challenges. The Bible reminds us in James 1:17, *"Every good and perfect gift is from above."* This means that the blessings we have come from God, and it is important to acknowledge and treasure them.

One way to cherish your blessings is by reflecting on them regularly. You can do this through practices like keeping a gratitude journal, where you write down things you are thankful for each day. This simple act helps you focus on the positive aspects of your life and deepens your appreciation for the blessings you might sometimes overlook. Additionally, sharing your gratitude with loved ones can strengthen relationships and spread joy and positivity among the people around you.

Cherishing your blessings isn't just about celebrating the big things in life. While big achievements and milestones deserve recognition, the small, everyday moments also bring comfort and joy. These small blessings — like a kind word from a friend, a sunny day, or a peaceful moment — are just as valuable. By appreciating these little things, you cultivate a mindset of gratitude that enriches your daily life and makes you more aware of God's presence in the ordinary.

When you cherish your blessings, it changes how you see life and gives you a greater sense of happiness and peace. Gratitude helps you to focus less on what you lack and more on what you already have. This perspective brings contentment and reduces stress. As 1 Thessalonians 5:18 says, *"Give thanks in all circumstances; for this is God's will for you in Christ Jesus."* By cherishing your blessings, you align your thoughts with God's will, which brings peace to your heart.

Finally, cherishing your blessings teaches you to share them with others. Recognizing the gifts you have received inspires you to give back and bless those around you. Whether it's offering words of encouragement, helping someone in need, or sharing your time and talents, appreciating your blessings encourages you to spread kindness. As you do this, you create a ripple effect of gratitude and love, making the world a better place. Cherishing your blessings isn't just about what you have—it's about using them to bring joy and positivity to others.

Train Your Heart to See Blessings

See the beauty in your life—because it's there. Sometimes we look at what we lack and forget what we have. We focus on the pain and miss the peace. But God has placed blessings all around you— some big, some small, all meaningful. The Bible says, *"Taste and see that the Lord is good; blessed is the one who takes refuge in Him"* (**Psalm 34:8**). You have breath in your lungs, strength in your spirit, and grace for each day. That's not little—it's a lot. You may not have everything you want, but you have more than enough to be thankful. When you open your eyes to what God has already given, you'll find joy in the journey. You'll see purpose in your past and hope in your future. Don't wait for perfect conditions to praise— praise in the present. Because beauty is not just in what you see— it's in how you see.

React to your blessings with gratitude and action. When God blesses you, He's not just giving you something—He's trusting you with something. Your response matters. Say "thank you," but also ask, "How can I use this to bless others?" The Bible says, *"From everyone who has been given much, much will be demanded"* (**Luke 12:48**). Gratitude should lead to generosity. Appreciation should lead to application. Don't just admire your blessings—activate them. Use your gifts to lift others. Share your story to strengthen someone else. Let your life be a light. When you respond with faith, you multiply the favor. When you react with purpose, you release power. So see the beauty, celebrate the blessing, and step into your calling.

Open Your Heart to What's Good

1. Precious

We should see our blessings as precious because they are gifts from God that hold great value. In James 1:17, the Bible says, *"Every good and perfect gift is from above, coming down from the Father of the heavenly lights."* This reminds us that our blessings are not random—they are carefully given to us by God out of His love and care. Cherishing our blessings helps us recognize their worth and fills our hearts with gratitude.

SYAVIHA MULENGYA

Our blessings are unique and tailored to our needs, making them even more special. Whether it's the people in our lives, opportunities, or simple joys, they all contribute to our happiness and growth. When we treat our blessings as precious, we align ourselves with God's purpose and show appreciation for His grace in our lives.

By seeing our blessings as treasures, we learn to protect and nurture them. This mindset helps us focus on the positive and embrace a grateful attitude. It reminds us that every blessing, big or small, is a sign of God's unfailing love and care for us.

2. Purposeful

Blessings are purposeful because they are given to us with intention and meaning. In Jeremiah 29:11, the Bible says, *"For I know the plans I have for you,"* declares the Lord, "plans to prosper you and not to harm you, plans to give you hope and a future." This verse highlights that God's blessings are part of His greater plan for our lives. They are meant to guide, encourage, and fulfill His purpose for us.

Recognizing the purpose of our blessings helps us use them wisely. When we understand that every gift has a reason, we can reflect on how to use them to glorify God and benefit others. Whether it's talents, opportunities, or relationships, each blessing plays a role in shaping our lives and spreading His love.

Living with the knowledge that our blessings have a purpose gives us a sense of direction and hope. It reminds us that God is intentional in everything He gives us, and He has a meaningful plan for our lives. This encourages us to trust Him and live in alignment with His will.

SYAVIHA MULENGYA

3. Powerful

Our blessings are powerful because they have the ability to transform lives and inspire change. In Philippians 4:13, it says, *"I can do all this through Him who gives me strength."* This verse shows that God's blessings equip us with the strength and ability to overcome challenges and achieve great things. His blessings empower us to rise above difficulties and reach our full potential.

When we embrace the power of our blessings, we find the courage and confidence to face life's challenges. God's gifts give us the tools to succeed and make an impact on those around us. Whether it's wisdom, skills, or resources, blessings are powerful because they enable us to accomplish what we couldn't do alone.

The transformative power of blessings also allows us to influence others positively. When we share our blessings and use them to serve others, we multiply their impact and bring God's love into the world. Acknowledging the power of blessings reminds us of the strength God has placed within us.

4. Privilege

We should look at our blessings as privileges because they are undeserved gifts of grace from God. In Romans 6:23, it says, *"The gift of God is eternal life in Christ Jesus our Lord."* This reminds us that blessings are not something we earn but are given freely by God out of His love for us. Treating blessings as privileges helps us remain humble and grateful for His generosity.

Seeing blessings as privileges also shifts our mindset to appreciation rather than entitlement. It teaches us to acknowledge God's goodness and kindness in our lives. When we recognize the privileges we have, we learn to handle them responsibly and honor Him through our actions.

SYAVIHA MULENGYA

A grateful attitude toward our blessings allows us to be mindful of their value and impact. It teaches us to focus on God's grace and share our blessings with those who may not have the same privileges, spreading His love and generosity.

5. Provision

Blessings are God's provision for our needs. In Philippians 4:19, it says, *"And my God will meet all your needs according to the riches of His glory in Christ Jesus."* This verse reminds us that God knows our needs and provides for us in ways that support and sustain us. Blessings are evidence of His care and faithfulness in our lives.

God's provision can come in many forms—physical, emotional, and spiritual. Whether it's food, shelter, comfort, or guidance, His blessings are meant to nurture us and help us grow. Seeing blessings as His provision encourages us to trust in His plan and rely on Him for all we need.

Recognizing blessings as provision also reminds us to be generous with what we have. God provides for us so we can share His love and care with others. By doing this, we honor His generosity and reflect His character to those around us.

6. Peaceful Our blessings bring peace to our lives, reminding us of God's love and protection. In John 14:27, Jesus says, *"Peace I leave with you; my peace I give you."* Blessings create a sense of calm and reassurance because they remind us that God is always with us. Cherishing these blessings helps us find peace even in challenging times.

When we look at our blessings as sources of peace, we focus on the comfort and stability they bring. Whether it's loving relationships, supportive communities, or personal achievements, blessings guide us toward harmony and balance in our lives.

SYAVIHA MULENGYA

The peace that comes from blessings encourages us to live in gratitude and faith. It helps us trust in God's plan and remain hopeful, knowing that He is always working for our good. This peace enriches our lives and deepens our connection with Him.

7. Personal and Public

Blessings are both personal and public because they benefit us individually while enabling us to bless others. In Genesis 12:2, God says, "*I will bless you... and you will be a blessing.*" This shows that blessings are not meant to be kept to ourselves but shared to bring joy and love to those around us.

Personal blessings, such as health, talents, and opportunities, enrich our lives and help us grow. Public blessings, like kindness and generosity, allow us to spread God's love and serve others. Recognizing both aspects of blessings encourages us to use them for good.

When we share our blessings, we create a ripple effect of positivity and gratitude. It transforms our individual gifts into communal blessings that build stronger relationships and communities. This reminds us that God's love is meant to be shared.

8. Potential

Blessings hold great potential because they are seeds of opportunity planted by God. In Ephesians 3:20, it says, "*Now to Him who is able to do immeasurably more than all we ask or imagine.*" Blessings are not just what we have—they represent what we can achieve with God's guidance and grace.

Looking at blessings as potential inspires us to dream and grow. Each blessing we receive is an opportunity to create something meaningful in our lives. Whether it's using our talents, resources, or relationships, God equips us to reach new heights.

By nurturing the potential of our blessings, we align ourselves with God's purpose and unlock possibilities we never imagined. This perspective encourages us to trust in His plans and make the most of what He has given us.

9. Prosperous

God's blessings lead us to prosperity, both spiritually and materially. In Jeremiah 29:11, it says, *"Plans to prosper you and not to harm you."* This verse reminds us that blessings are part of God's plan to bring abundance into our lives. Prosperity through blessings is not just about wealth—it's about spiritual growth, joy, and fulfillment.

When we look at blessings as sources of prosperity, we see how they enrich every area of our lives. They help us achieve goals, strengthen relationships, and deepen our connection with God. Prosperity through blessings reflects His goodness and faithfulness.

Recognizing the prosperity of blessings also encourages us to share them. By giving back and helping others, we multiply their impact and create a cycle of abundance rooted in God's love.

10. Positive

Blessings are inherently positive because they represent the good things God brings into our lives. In Romans 8:28, it says, *"And we know that in all things God works for the good of those who love Him."* Seeing blessings as positive helps us focus on gratitude instead of negativity, lifting our spirits and renewing our faith.

Looking at blessings as positive encourages us to celebrate the good moments, even during difficult times. This perspective helps us stay hopeful and trust in God's plan, knowing that He is working for our benefit.

The positivity of blessings also inspires us to spread joy and kindness to others. By focusing on the good in our lives, we become a source of encouragement and hope for those around us, reflecting God's love in all we do.

13

GROW WITH GRATITUDE AND GOODNESS

To grow with goodness is to choose a life of depth, direction, and divine purpose. It means becoming more than what we were yesterday—more grateful, more gracious, more grounded. Growth is not just about gaining knowledge or achieving success; it's about becoming a person of character, compassion, and conviction. Goodness is the fruit of a heart aligned with God's will and a life committed to truth. When we grow with gratitude, we begin to see blessings in every season. When we grow with grace, we learn to forgive, to heal, and to walk humbly. When we grow with generosity, we become vessels of hope and healing to those around us. Greatness is not measured by status, but by service. Goals give us direction, but goodness gives us depth. God's guidance keeps us on the path of righteousness. Giving is not just an act—it's a lifestyle of love. And glory belongs not to us, but to the One who empowers our growth.

Growing with goodness requires intentionality, humility, and spiritual discipline. It means choosing prayer over pride, SYAVIHA MULENGYA productivity over passivity, and purpose over pressure. It's about living a life that reflects the heart of God in every word, every action, and every relationship. Goodness is not perfection—it's progress powered by grace. It's the quiet strength that lifts others, the gentle wisdom that speaks truth, and the steady faith that endures storms. To grow with goodness is to be rooted in love and ready to serve. It's to be grounded in truth and guided by vision. It's about living with integrity, walking with humility, and leading with compassion. Growth is not a destination—it's a daily decision. Every moment is an opportunity to choose kindness, courage, and clarity. When we grow with goodness, we build lives that are fruitful, faithful, and full of grace. And in doing so, we reflect the light of Christ to a world in need of hope.

Believe You Are Blessed

To grow with gratitude, you must first believe you are blessed. Your belief shapes your behavior, your attitude, and your actions. **Proverbs 23:7** says, *"As he thinks in his heart, so is he."* If you believe you are favored by God, you will walk with confidence and peace. When you believe you are chosen, you stop chasing approval and start living with purpose. Gratitude begins with a mindset that sees God's hand in every moment. You are not forgotten—you are favored. You are not empty—you are equipped. **Jeremiah 29:11** reminds us that God has good plans for you. Believing this truth helps you rise with hope and rest with assurance. Gratitude grows when you stop doubting and start declaring. Say it daily: "I am blessed, I am useful, I am growing."

Your belief becomes your foundation. It gives you the strength to face challenges and the courage to pursue your calling. When you believe you are blessed, you stop shrinking and start shining. You begin to speak with boldness and serve with joy. Gratitude flows from a heart that knows its worth. You are not defined by your past—you are refined by God's grace. **Philippians 4:8** tells us to think on what is true, noble, and praiseworthy. Fill your mind with faith, not fear. Fill your heart with hope, not hurt. Gratitude grows when you believe that God is working, even when you don't see it. Your belief shapes your future. And your future is full of favor.

1. Recognize What You Have

Gratitude grows when you recognize what you already have. Many people have blessings but don't see them. They have peace but don't enjoy it. They have a purpose but don't pursue it. **Psalm 139:14** says, *"I am fearfully and wonderfully made."* You are God's masterpiece, created with gifts, grace, and greatness. Take time to reflect on your talents, your relationships, and your opportunities. What you have is not little—it's a lot. Don't overlook your blessings—observe them. Don't downplay your worth—declare it. Gratitude begins when you stop looking at what's missing and start thanking God for what's present. You are rich in love, strong in spirit, and full of potential.

When you recognize your blessings, your perspective changes. You stop comparing and start celebrating. You stop complaining and start appreciating. Gratitude helps you see your life through the lens of love, not lack. It reminds you that every good thing is a gift from God. You are not behind—you are becoming. You are not broken—you are being built. Gratitude helps you honor your journey and embrace your growth. It teaches you to say, "Thank You, Lord," even when things are hard. When you recognize what you have, you become more grounded and grateful. And when you're grateful, you grow in goodness.

SYAVIHA MULENGYA

2. Receive the Blessing

To grow in gratitude, you must be willing to receive what God gives. Many people block their blessings because they feel unworthy or afraid. But **James 1:17** reminds us, *"Every good and perfect gift is from above."* God doesn't bless you because you're perfect—He blesses you because He's faithful. Receiving is not just about taking—it's about trusting. It's saying, "Lord, I accept Your favor, Your grace, and Your goodness." When you receive with humility, you make room for more. You begin to walk in joy, live in peace, and serve with purpose. Gratitude grows when you stop rejecting your worth and start receiving your assignment. Don't say, "It's just a little"—say, "It's already a lot." What you receive today is preparation for what you'll release tomorrow.

Receiving also means recognizing that blessings come in many forms. Sometimes they arrive as opportunities, relationships, or lessons. Sometimes they come wrapped in challenges that stretch your faith. But every blessing is a seed for growth. When you receive with an open heart, you allow God to do more in you and through you. You stop resisting and start rejoicing. You stop doubting and start developing. Gratitude helps you welcome what God sends, even when it's unexpected. It teaches you to say, "Thank You," before you see the full picture. Receiving is not weakness—it's wisdom. It's how you grow with grace and walk in goodness.

3. Rejoice in the Blessing

Gratitude grows when you rejoice in what God has done. **Philippians 4:4** says, *"Rejoice in the Lord always. I will say it again: Rejoice!"* Rejoicing is not just for good days—it's for every day. It's a decision to celebrate even when life feels uncertain. When you rejoice, you release joy. You shift your focus from problems to

SYAVIHA MULENGYA

praise. You stop groaning and start glowing. You stop worrying and start worshiping. Gratitude helps you find joy in the journey, not just the destination. It helps you dance in the rain and sing in the storm. Rejoicing is a spiritual weapon—it lifts your spirit and strengthens your faith.

Rejoicing also reminds you of God's faithfulness. It helps you remember the victories, the answered prayers, and the quiet miracles. It builds your confidence and fuels your hope. When you rejoice, you reflect God's goodness to others. You become a light in dark places and a voice of encouragement. Gratitude grows when you celebrate the small wins and honor the big ones. Rejoicing is not noise—it's nourishment. It feeds your soul and refreshes your heart. It helps you stay positive, peaceful, and powerful. When you rejoice, you grow stronger. And when you grow stronger, you grow in gratitude and goodness.

4. Rely on God

To grow with gratitude, you must rely on God completely. **Proverbs 3:5-6** says, *"Trust in the Lord with all your heart and lean not on your own understanding."* God is your source, your strength, and your stability. When you rely on Him, you stop leaning on your own wisdom. You stop stressing and start surrendering. You stop panicking and start praying. Gratitude grows when you trust the Giver more than the gift. It helps you walk by faith, not by fear. It helps you rest in God's promises, even when life feels uncertain. Relying on God means saying, "Lord, I trust You even when I don't understand." That trust becomes your anchor in every storm.

Relying on God also means letting go of control. It means submitting your plans, your dreams, and your decisions to Him. When you rely on God, you receive peace that passes understanding. You receive strength that sustains you. You receive

SYAVIHA MULENGYA

wisdom that guides you. Gratitude grows when you stop trying to fix everything and start trusting God with everything. It helps you live with confidence, not confusion. It helps you move forward with purpose, not pressure. Relying on God is not weakness—it's worship. It's how you grow deeper in faith and stronger in spirit. And when you rely on Him, you walk in goodness every day.

5. Remain Humble and Happy

Gratitude grows in hearts that are humble. Humility helps you remember that everything you have is a gift from God. **1 Peter 5:6** says, *"Humble yourselves, therefore, under God's mighty hand, that He may lift you up in due time."* When you stay grounded, you stay grateful. You stop boasting and start blessing. You stop demanding and start depending. Humility helps you appreciate your blessings without taking them for granted. It reminds you that success is not self-made—it's God-given. Gratitude flows when you know you didn't earn it, but you received it. Humble people are thankful people. They honor God with their attitude and actions. And that honor leads to elevation.

Happiness is the fruit of a grateful heart. When you choose joy, you choose strength. **Nehemiah 8:10** says, *"The joy of the Lord is your strength."* Happiness doesn't come from having everything—it comes from appreciating everything. You find joy in the little things, the quiet moments, and the daily mercies. Gratitude helps you smile more, stress less, and shine brighter. When you remain humble and happy, you create an atmosphere of peace and positivity. You become a light in your home, your workplace, and your community. Gratitude teaches you to laugh, to love, and to live fully. It helps you carry joy into every room and every relationship. Humility keeps you grounded. Happiness keeps you glowing. Together, they help you grow in goodness.

SYAVIHA MULENGYA

6. Remember God Is the Source

Gratitude grows when you remember where your blessings come from. **Deuteronomy 8:18** says, *"But remember the Lord your God, for it is He who gives you the ability to produce wealth."* Your job is not your source—God is. Your talent is not your provider—God is. When you keep God at the center, you stay connected to the flow of favor. You stop chasing and start cherishing. You stop striving and start surrendering. Gratitude helps you see that every good thing is a gift from above. It reminds you to give thanks, not just for what you have, but for who gave it. God is your provider, your protector, and your peace. When you remember Him, you remain rooted. And when you're rooted, you grow strong.

Remembering God as your source also keeps you humble and hopeful. It helps you avoid pride and embrace praise. You stop saying, "I did this," and start saying, "God did this." You begin to live with open hands and an open heart. You become more generous, more joyful, and more gentle. Gratitude grows when you give God credit for your progress. It helps you stay thankful in success and faithful in struggle. You remember that He is your beginning, your builder, and your breakthrough. When you keep your eyes on Him, you walk in wisdom. You live with purpose, peace, and power. And you grow with gratitude and goodness every step of the way.

7. Reject Doubt and Fear

Gratitude cannot grow in the soil of fear. **Isaiah 41:10** says, *"Do not fear... I will strengthen you and help you."* Doubt drains your joy. Fear blocks your faith. But gratitude builds your belief. It helps you focus on what is true, noble, and praiseworthy (**Philippians 4:8**). When you reject fear, you make room for faith. When you reject doubt, you make room for destiny. Gratitude helps you see God's hand even in hard times. It reminds you that you are not alone, not forgotten, and not finished. You are blessed, you are chosen, and you are growing. Fear fades when faith rises.

Rejecting doubt and fear is a daily decision. It means choosing to trust God even when you don't understand. It means saying, "I believe," even when you feel uncertain. Gratitude helps you stay focused on God's promises, not your problems. It helps you walk with courage, speak with confidence, and live with clarity. You stop worrying and start worshiping. You stop hesitating and start hoping. Gratitude is your shield against negativity. It protects your peace and powers your progress. When you reject fear, you release favor. When you reject doubt, you receive direction. And that's how you grow—with gratitude in your heart and goodness in your steps.

Grow strong

1. Purpose – Know Why You Exist

Goodness begins with clarity. When you understand your God-given purpose, you live with direction, not distraction. Purpose gives your life meaning and your actions weight. It helps you rise above confusion and focus on what truly matters. Without purpose, life feels random and reactive. But with purpose, every step becomes intentional and impactful. You were created for a reason, and your existence is not an accident. *"For we are God's handiwork, created in Christ Jesus to do good works..."* (**Ephesians 2:10**). God designed you with gifts, dreams, and a mission to fulfill. Your purpose is tied to your identity and your calling. It's not just about what you do—it's about who you become. When you walk in purpose, you walk in power.

2. Plan – Walk with Intention

A good life doesn't happen by accident. Planning helps you align your time, energy, and resources with your values. A plan

SYAVIHA MULENGYA

turns your purpose into progress. It gives structure to your dreams and clarity to your decisions. Without a plan, even the best intentions can drift. Planning is a form of stewardship—it honors the time and talents God has given you. It helps you stay focused and avoid distractions. A wise plan includes prayer, priorities, and preparation. *"Commit to the Lord whatever you do, and he will establish your plans."* (**Proverbs 16:3**). It's not rigid, but responsive to God's guidance. Planning helps you live with excellence, not just effort. When you plan with God, you walk in peace and confidence.

3. Principles – Stand on Truth

Growing with goodness means living by unshakable values. Principles protect your character and guide your decisions. They help you stay grounded when the world feels unstable. Honesty, humility, integrity, and love are not just ideals—they are anchors. Principles shape your reputation and reflect your relationship with God. They help you choose what's right over what's easy. When you live by truth, you build trust. *"The integrity of the upright guides them..."* (**Proverbs 11:3**). Principles give you courage to stand firm in storms. They help you lead with consistency and serve with sincerity. A principled life is a powerful witness. Goodness grows when truth is your foundation.

4. Passion – Fuel Your Fire

Passion gives your purpose energy. It's the joy, excitement, and drive that keep you going when things get tough. Passion makes your goodness contagious. It inspires others and ignites hope. When you serve with passion, you bring life to your mission. Passion is not noise—it's depth, devotion, and determination. It helps you persevere through challenges and celebrate small victories. Passion flows from love—love for God, for people, and for your calling. *"Never be lacking in zeal, but keep your spiritual fervor, serving the Lord."* (**Romans 12:11**). It's the spark that turns routine into revival. Passion keeps your heart engaged and your spirit alive. When you lose passion, you lose momentum.

5. Proactive – Take Initiative

Don't wait for change—be the change. Growing with goodness means stepping up, speaking out, and serving others without being asked. It's about leading with love and living with purpose. A proactive person doesn't just react—they respond with wisdom and courage. They see needs and meet them. They don't wait for permission to do good. Being proactive means taking responsibility for your growth and your impact. It's choosing action over apathy. It's being intentional with your time, your words, and your influence. *"Do not merely listen to the word... Do what it says."* (**James 1:22**). Proactive people build bridges, solve problems, and create opportunities. Goodness grows when you move with boldness and compassion.

6. Potential – Believe in What's Possible

God placed greatness in you. Growing with goodness means recognizing your gifts and stretching beyond your comfort zone. You were made for more than survival—you were made for significance. Potential is the promise of what can be when you trust God and take action. It's not about perfection—it's about progress. Your potential is unlocked through faith, effort, and obedience. Don't let fear shrink your future. Believe in what God says about you, not what doubt whispers. *"I can do all things through Christ who strengthens me."* (**Philippians 4:13**). You have talents waiting to be developed and dreams waiting to be pursued. When you grow your potential, you expand your impact. Goodness flourishes when you believe in what's possible.

7. Prayer – Stay Connected to the Source

Prayer is the power line of goodness. It keeps your heart soft, your spirit strong, and your focus clear. Prayer aligns your will with God's and fills you with peace. It's not just a ritual—it's a relationship. Prayer invites God into your plans, your pain, and your progress. It strengthens your faith and renews your mind. Through prayer, you receive wisdom, comfort, and courage. It's where battles are fought and victories are won. Prayer helps you stay humble and hopeful. *"Devote yourselves to prayer, being watchful and thankful."* (**Colossians 4:2**). It's the secret to spiritual strength and emotional stability. Goodness grows when you stay connected to the Source.

8. Productivity – Bear Fruit That Lasts

Goodness isn't just about intentions—it's about impact. Productivity means using your time wisely, serving others, and producing results that glorify God. It's not about being busy—it's about being effective. Fruitful living is focused living. Productivity flows from purpose, planning, and prayer. It helps you turn ideas into action and values into victories. A productive life blesses others and honors God. It's marked by diligence, discipline, and discernment. Productivity is not just what you do—it's what you become through consistent effort. *"By this my Father is glorified, that you bear much fruit..."* (**John 15:8**). When you bear fruit, you build a legacy. Goodness multiplies when you live with intention and excellence.

SYAVIHA MULENGYA

14

GRATITUDE LEADS TO MORE BLESSINGS

Gratitude is a spiritual key that unlocks the door to deeper joy, peace, and provision. When we choose to be thankful, we shift our focus from what's missing to what's meaningful. This shift in perspective helps us recognize the blessings we already have, which often go unnoticed in the rush of daily life. Gratitude is not just a feeling—it's a decision to honor God with our attitude. Scripture reminds us, *"Give thanks in all circumstances; for this is God's will for you in Christ Jesus"* (**1 Thessalonians 5:18**). When we obey this command, we position ourselves to receive more of what God wants to give. A thankful heart is humble, receptive, and full of faith. It acknowledges that every good gift comes from above and that God is always working, even when we don't understand. Gratitude doesn't change our circumstances immediately, but it changes how we experience them. And when our hearts are aligned with heaven, blessings begin to multiply.

SYAVIHA MULENGYA

Jesus modeled this principle when He fed the five thousand. Before the miracle happened, He took the five loaves and two fish and *"gave thanks"* (**John 6:11**). That act of gratitude preceded the multiplication. It wasn't the size of the offering—it was the spirit of thanksgiving that invited divine increase. Gratitude turns scarcity into sufficiency and lack into abundance. When we thank God for what we have, we open the door for Him to do more with it. This applies not only to resources but also to relationships, opportunities, and spiritual growth. A grateful heart is a fertile ground for miracles. It says, "Lord, I trust You with what I have, and I believe You can do more." Gratitude is the seed—blessing is the harvest.

Gratitude also strengthens our relationships and builds emotional resilience. When we express appreciation to others, we affirm their value and deepen our connection. Saying "thank you" is more than manners—it's ministry. It heals wounds, restores trust, and creates a culture of honor. **Proverbs 17:22** says, *"A cheerful heart is good medicine, but a crushed spirit dries up the bones."* Gratitude brings cheerfulness, which in turn brings healing. It helps us see people not through the lens of frustration, but through the lens of grace. When we're grateful for others, we become more patient, more forgiving, and more joyful. Gratitude transforms how we relate to others—and that transformation invites blessing into our homes, workplaces, and communities.

Gratitude also prepares us to be good stewards of what we've been given. When we appreciate what we have, we take better care of it. We stop comparing and start cultivating. Gratitude helps us see our resources as gifts, not burdens. It teaches us to manage with joy, not with complaint. **Luke 16:10** says, *"Whoever can be trusted with very little can also be trusted with much."* A grateful person is trustworthy because they value what's in their hands.

SYAVIHA MULENGYA

They don't waste time wishing for more—they maximize what they already have. And as they prove faithful, God entrusts them with greater responsibility and reward. Gratitude is the foundation of stewardship—and stewardship leads to increase.

Gratitude draws us closer to God and deepens our spiritual intimacy. **Psalm 100:4** says, *"Enter his gates with thanksgiving and his courts with praise."* Thanksgiving is the gateway to God's presence. When we come before Him with a grateful heart, we experience His peace, His joy, and His power. Gratitude is worship—it's a declaration that God is good, even when life is hard. It reminds us that we are not alone and that His grace is sufficient. A grateful heart is a surrendered heart, one that trusts God's timing and treasures His presence. Gratitude doesn't just lead to external blessings—it leads to internal transformation. It changes how we pray, how we live, and how we love. And in that transformation, we find the greatest blessing of all: closeness with the One who gives every good and perfect gift.

Do you want more, be gratitude

Gratitude has the power to transform our lives and increase our blessings. It shifts our hearts toward recognizing and appreciating the gifts God has given us. In the story of the ten lepers in Luke 17:11-19, only one of them returned to give thanks to Jesus. He not only received healing but was forgiven of his sins. This illustrates how gratitude deepens our connection with God and opens the door for greater blessings. When we give thanks, we please God, and He continues to pour out His goodness in our lives.

Gratitude is not just about acknowledging blessings—it's about choosing to focus on the good even when life is difficult. As 1 Thessalonians 5:18 teaches, *"Give thanks in all circumstances; for this is God's will for you in Christ Jesus."* When we cultivate

SYAVIHA MULENGYA

gratitude, it helps us discover, develop, dedicate, share, delight in, and direct our blessings. Let us explore these ways in which gratitude multiplies the good in our lives.

1. Discover Our Blessings. Gratitude helps us recognize the blessings in our lives that we might otherwise overlook. It shifts our perspective, allowing us to see the goodness of God in the little things, such as good health, relationships, and opportunities. The Bible in James 1:17 reminds us, *"Every good and perfect gift is from above."* Reflecting on this verse encourages us to take time to discover the gifts God has placed around us, even in moments of challenge.

When we practice gratitude, we become more aware of God's presence and provision. It teaches us to look beyond the struggles and appreciate the blessings hidden in the everyday. This awareness brings joy and contentment, helping us to focus on the abundance in our lives. Gratitude opens our eyes to all that God has done for us, deepening our faith and trust in Him.

2. Develop Our Blessings. Gratitude motivates us to develop and nurture the blessings we have been given. By thanking God for our talents, relationships, and resources, we are inspired to use them wisely and faithfully. In Matthew 25:21, Jesus says, *"You have been faithful with a few things; I will put you in charge of many things."* Gratitude encourages us to steward our blessings, allowing them to grow and flourish.

When we focus on developing our blessings, we honor God and align ourselves with His purpose. Whether it's learning new skills, strengthening relationships, or taking care of our health, gratitude helps us see the potential in what we have. This mindset leads to growth and prosperity, making the most of God's gifts while giving Him glory.

SYAVIHA MULENGYA

3. Dedicate Our Blessings. Gratitude leads us to dedicate our blessings to God as an act of worship and trust. By acknowledging that our gifts come from Him, we honor Him and invite Him to use them for His glory. In Romans 12:1, it says, *"Offer your bodies as a living sacrifice, holy and pleasing to God—this is your true and proper worship."* Dedicating our blessings helps us align them with His will.

When we dedicate our blessings to God, we deepen our relationship with Him and find greater purpose in what we have. It reminds us that everything we possess is part of His plan, and by surrendering it to Him, we allow Him to work through us. Gratitude transforms our blessings into tools for fulfilling His purpose.

4. Distribute Our Blessings. Gratitude teaches us to share our blessings with others. By recognizing how much we have received, we are motivated to be generous and help those in need. In Genesis 12:2, God says, *"I will bless you... and you will be a blessing."* Sharing our blessings reflects His love and creates a ripple effect of kindness and joy.

When we distribute our blessings, we strengthen relationships and build a sense of community. Whether it's giving time, resources, or encouragement, sharing allows us to multiply the impact of our blessings. Gratitude reminds us that we are not meant to keep our gifts to ourselves but to use them to make a difference in the lives of others.

5. Delight in Our Blessings. Gratitude helps us take joy in the blessings we have received. It encourages us to celebrate the goodness of God and find contentment in His provision. In Psalm 37:4, it says, *"Take delight in the Lord, and He will give you the desires of your heart."* Gratitude brings a sense of happiness and peace as we enjoy the abundance God has provided.

SYAVIHA MULENGYA

Delighting in our blessings also deepens our trust in God's faithfulness. It reminds us to appreciate the present and let go of worries about the future. Gratitude turns our focus from what we lack to the fullness of what God has already given us, bringing joy and fulfillment.

6. Direct Our Blessings. Gratitude helps us use our blessings purposefully and wisely. By thanking God for what we have, we seek His guidance in how to use it. In Proverbs 3:6, it says, "In all your ways submit to Him, and He will make your paths straight." Gratitude encourages us to trust God's plan for our blessings and follow His direction.

When we direct our blessings, we ensure that they are used for good and to glorify God. This intentionality gives our gifts greater meaning and allows us to fulfill His purpose for our lives. Gratitude keeps us focused on His will, ensuring that our blessings are used in ways that honor Him and benefit others.

Gratitude is more than an emotion—it's a powerful tool that helps us discover, develop, dedicate, share, delight in, and direct our blessings. By practicing gratitude, we open our hearts to God's goodness and invite Him to multiply His blessings in our lives. Let us be thankful for all He has done and trust Him for even greater things.

Prayer to Grow with Gratitude and Goodness

Heavenly Father, thank You for Your love, Your grace, and Your goodness. You have blessed me more than I deserve and more than I often recognize. Help me to see the beauty in my life and the blessings in every moment. Teach me to be grateful in every season—when things are easy and when they are hard. Let my heart overflow with thanksgiving, not just in words but in actions.

SYAVIHA MULENGYA

Help me to grow in goodness, to reflect Your character in how I live, love, and lead. Make me a vessel of kindness, a voice of hope, and a light in dark places. Let my gratitude lead me to generosity, and my joy lead me to service. Keep me humble, happy, and hungry for more of You. May I never forget that You are my source, my strength, and my sustainer. I choose to grow with gratitude and walk in Your goodness, today and every day. In Jesus' name, Amen.

Prayer of Repentance

Merciful Father, I come before You with a humble heart, asking for Your forgiveness. Forgive me for the times I've complained instead of giving thanks. Forgive me for the moments I've doubted Your plan and feared the future. Cleanse my heart from pride, bitterness, and unbelief. Renew my mind with Your truth and restore my spirit with Your peace. Help me to turn away from anything that dishonors You. I repent of every wrong thought, word, and action. Create in me a clean heart, O God, and renew a right spirit within me. Let Your grace wash over me and Your mercy lift me up. Thank You for loving me even when I fall short. Thank You for giving me a new chance to walk in Your will. I receive Your forgiveness and choose to live in Your light. In Jesus' name, Amen.

By SYAVIHA MULENGYA